The Bond King

Investment Secrets from PIMCO's Bill Gross

Timothy Middleton

WILEY

John Wiley & Sons, Inc.

Published by John Wiley & Sons, Inc., Hoboken, New Jersey.
Published simultaneously in Canada.

For general information on our other products and services, or technical support, please contact our Customer Care Department within the United States at 800-762-2974, outside the United States at 317-572-3993 or fax 317-572-4002.

Wiley also publishes its books in a variety of electronic formats. Some content that appears in print may not be available in electronic books.

For additional information about Wiley products, visit our web site at www.wiley.com.

Library of Congress Cataloging-in-Publication Data

Middleton, Timothy.
   The bond king : investment secrets from PIMCO's Bill Gross / Timothy Middleton.
     p.   cm.
  ISBN: 0-471-46254-3 (CLOTH)
  1. Bonds. 2. Bond market. 3. Investments. 4. Gross, William H. I. Title.
HG4651 .M53 2004
332.63′23—dc22

          2003022632

Printed in the United States of America

10 9 8 7 6 5 4 3 2 1

Contents

Foreword

Where It All Began

We all know what the oldest profession is, but few of us know enough about one of the youngest professions; the art and science of active bond management. Although PIMCO and Bill Gross are the primary focus of this book, its compelling story of active management of fixed-income portfolios reaches far beyond PIMCO's remarkable track record and Bill Gross's powerful leadership. Fixed-income management is fascinating, complex, essential to our economic system, and a great way to grow your wealth—if you know what you are doing. Yet many investors in these markets understand much less about fixed-income fundamentals than they should, which puts them in the same class as the millions of innocents who have been fleeced time and again in the stock market.

Indeed, until about thirty years ago, the lender handed the money over to the borrower and then collected interest until the borrower repaid the loan. That was all there was to it. The notion that anyone might routinely *trade* these instruments by selling them to other investors prior to maturity did not exist. The polite and conservative society of bondholders—primarily insurance companies, savings banks, personal trusts, and retired people of wealth—would have shunned such a drastic step as something not quite acceptable. There was modest activity in government securities, a limited number of big-name credits listed on the New York Stock Exchange, and a quiet over-the-counter market on the side.

The interesting question is why bond trading took so long to develop. Mispriced assets are just as likely to occur in credit markets as anywhere else. There is no good reason why the original pricing of the deal should be immutable through the life of the loan. Neither the particulars of each situation nor the fundamental economic environment is likely to stand still. The quality of a credit will change as the borrower's financial position shifts over time. Bonds frequently include options, such as call provisions or convertibility into equity securities, and their prices should fluctuate with the value of these options. Volatility patterns are also unstable.

Finally, the biggest and most tenacious enemy of lenders is inflation, the chance that the money repaid will not buy as much as the money originally lent. But until the 1960s, inflation had been only a wartime phenomenon that disappeared the instant the peace treaties were signed. Inflation in the United States from 1800 to 1965 averaged merely 0.8 percent a year; prices rose in only 84 out of those 165 years, which included fourteen years when the country was at war. The relaxed outlook for inflation over that very long time span was the primary factor in persuading lenders that a buy-and-hold strategy was best for their business.

The bond market was such a sleepy place that even the theory of interest rates developed at a remarkably slow pace. The classical economists of the nineteenth century believed that interest, like all prices, was determined by the immutable laws of supply and demand. If interest was the price of capital, then the supply of saving and the demand from business firms for investment would be its primary determinants. This was a simple paradigm suggesting only modest volatility in interest rates.

In 1930, the distinguished Yale economist Irving Fisher introduced the idea that interest rates reflect expectations of inflation as well as the supply and demand for real capital. This was a remarkable insight in view of the absence of any kind of structural inflation in American or English economic history up to that time, but Fisher pressed the point even though empirical support for his hypothesis was lacking.

In the depths of the Great Depression, John Maynard Keynes launched a powerful attack on the classical view of the "real" rate of interest, in which he included Fisher. Keynes emphasized the critically important role of the cost of capital in business decisions to invest in plant and equipment. However, he insisted that the rate of interest was determined not by the supply and demand of capital or even by inflation expectations but as a kind of risk management tool, ruled by the demand for liquidity from risk-averse investors in an uncertain world relative to the supply of liquidity provided by the banking system.

In 1938, Frederick R. Macaulay's magisterial book on the bond market, commodity prices, and stock prices launched a bitter attack on Fisher (Macaulay, a personal friend of mine, told me Keynes was not worth the trouble), focusing mercilessly on the weak empirical support up to that time for Fisher's case. There were too many irregularities in the historical statistics to satisfy Macaulay. Yet Fisher ultimately turned out to be right about the impact of inflation expectations on interest rates, as peacetime inflation became an increasingly serious challenge in economies around the world during the late 1960s and the 1970s.

We must be grateful to Macaulay nevertheless: He provided a critically important innovation while shaping his argument against Fisher. Macaulay recognized he had to build his case from the foundation of a meticulous definition of the long-term interest rate. As he worked through that definition, he noted that a bond's maturity date, while important, did not necessarily identify the moment when lenders would have their principal back. Simple interest at 6 percent would return the original investment in less than seventeen years even though a bond might have a maturity of twenty years; by reinvesting the semiannual coupons of 3 percent, investors would earn enough additional interest to have their money back even sooner. Accordingly, Macaulay proposed the concept of duration, which, in a general sense, measures the length of time required before the cash flows of interest and principal paid by the borrower equal the amount of money originally provided by the lender. As a bonus, duration turned out to be a strategic element in assessing the volatility of bond prices in response to changes in interest rates. Today, Macaulay's definition of duration is the basic metric of risk in the bond market.

Yet the bond market itself remained somnolent until the mid-1960s, more than fifteen years after World War II, when inflation began to creep up from a range of 1 percent to 2 percent a year to annual rates of more than 2 percent and soon to more than 3 percent. By 1968, as inflation surpassed 4 percent, the price level was no longer just creeping upward; by 1970, prices were climbing at an annual rate of 6 percent. Fixed-income investors were finally beginning to get the point. As the yield on long-term Treasury bonds climbed along with the rate of inflation, the prices of outstanding bonds sank ever more deeply. Soon the bitter words "certificates of confiscation" became the popular phrase to describe bonds—once upon a time considered the safest investment anyone could make.

Consider the case of an investor in 1965 who invested $100,000 in a 30-year bond priced at 100 with a promised yield of 4 percent. Fifteen years later, the price of this bond would have fallen to 45, or $450 for each $1,000 invested. As inflation took its terrible toll, that $450 would have been able to buy less than 40 percent of what $450 could have bought in 1954. Buy-and-hold appeared to make less and less sense. The bond market would never be the same.

In 1972, when the most serious damage was still in the future, a slim new volume on bond investing set the tempo for active bond management to become a reality—indeed, a necessity. Written by two Salomon Brothers economists, Sidney Homer and Martin Leibowitz, *Inside the Yield Curve* finally awakened bond portfolio managers to the complexity of their fixed-income instruments and the trading opportunities that complexity provided. The book was in many ways a primer whose lessons today are taken for granted, but few people at the time were aware of its importance. As the authors point out in their very first paragraph, "Too often the dollars and cents significance of bond yields is taken for granted and sometimes even misunderstood."

For example, the mathematics underlying the calculation of a bond's yield to maturity assumes that the semiannual interest payments, or coupons, are reinvested at the same rate as the promised yield on the bond at the time of purchase. Such an outcome would be a rare coincidence. When interest rates averaged 2 percent or even 3 percent, the interest rate at which bondholders reinvested their coupon income made little difference. But reinvesting coupons of 6 percent or more on a bond with a life of over twenty years is something else entirely. Now you are talking about real money, sums that could exceed the original amount of the principal lent. You are also invoking the power of compound interest—"interest-on-interest" as Homer and Leibowitz dubbed it—making this extra source of return a dominant factor in the investor's ultimate payoff.

The book goes on to explain volatility in bond prices, a phenomenon that nobody had to bother about in the good old days but one that is now a source of opportunity as well as risk. To cap their story, Homer and Leibowitz describe in detail the kinds of trading in the bond market—"bond swaps"—that could turn a profit for the active and analytically inclined investor.

At about the same time as the appearance of the Homer-Leibowitz book, a few intrepid investment professionals decided to try their hand at developing active management strategies, based on widespread mispricing of bonds as most investors hung on to their longstanding policy of buy-and-hold in an increasingly unstable environment. The darkening outlook for inflation and the bond market's rising volatility offered a wide variety of new opportunities. These pioneers soon built up enviable track records from sophisticated interest rate and yield curve forecasting as well as from the plethora of inefficiencies provided by a notably illiquid marketplace. The profession of active fixed-income management was born.

Among these pioneers was a West Coast insurance company called Pacific Mutual (now Pacific Life), which early on undertook active fixed-income management in its own portfolio. In 1971, it established a subsidiary called PIMCO to carry out the mission of active management for clients. Bill Gross was there right at the start: His first job out of UCLA business school was with PIMCO.

The rest is history, well told in the pages that follow.

Peter L. Bernstein
November 2003

Preface

Bill Gross spends a certain amount of time looking at the world upside down, literally—he practices yoga. He refuses to pay attention to the conventional wisdom in life and in business, and over his legendary thirty-year investing career, this perspective has paid off. Gross manages $360 billion in fixed income assets and has consistently delivered returns averaging more than 10 percent annually.

What sets Gross apart from his peers is vision. Before almost anyone else, he realized that bond investing held untapped opportunity. Perhaps Gross's greatest contribution to the investment industry is the insight that a fixed-income portfolio can be traded, rather than just held, and that this kind of active management increases total returns. Gross introduced this concept of total returns to bond investing, and today, he manages the world's largest actively managed mutual fund, and its name says it all: PIMCO Total Return Fund.

This is the story of a remarkable investor who himself once thought of bonds as being boring. Gross did not set out to become the

Bond King, but he has undoubtedly become *the* master of this investment universe. The attribution "Bond King" quickly categorizes Gross, but the details of his investment philosophy and approach depict a complex individual who is nothing short of fascinating.

In 1982, Gross wrote an article in PIMCO's "Investment Outlook" newsletter, a publication sent to the firm's clients, that I found particularly telling. In the piece, entitled "Hedgehog Time," a reference to Sir Isaiah Berlin's essay "The Hedgehog and the Fox," Gross explains his secular, or long-range, vision of investing by analogy to the hedgehog. "The fox knows many things, but the hedgehog knows one big thing," Berlin had written, quoting the aphorism of the ancient Greek poet Archilochus. Gross cast the market as a fox, constantly chasing after the latest thing to catch its eye, and himself as the hedgehog, focused on the big, long-range picture. In 1982 the market had not yet seized on Paul Volcker's new anti-inflation reality. It was looking back at the prior decade's bear market in bonds. Gross was looking ahead to what he predicted would be a new bull market in the 1980s. He was correct in his prediction because he was correct in his vision, which itself derived from the focused, dedicated effort that he puts into understanding the world around him.

Berlin's essay aptly defines the characteristics I find so compelling about Gross. "There exists," Berlin wrote, "a great chasm between those, on one side, who relate everything to a single central vision, one system less or more coherent or articulate, in terms of which they understand, think and feel—a single, universal, organizing principle in terms of which alone all that they are and say has significance—and, on the other side, those who pursue many ends, often unrelated and even contradictory, connected, if at all, only in some *de facto* way, for some psychological or physiological cause, related by no moral or aesthetic principle." Gross is a hedgehog, and not a bad philosopher.

This book, then, is about Bill Gross's professional life and what we can learn from his experiences and investment strategies. As such, there is little mention of his life as a husband and father. However, these are the roles of which he is proudest. His first marriage ended in the early, time-crushing years of his career, and when he remarried 19 years ago he made a commitment to devote more of himself to his family. These days those who read his newsletter regularly have come to know his wife, Sue, and his teenage son, Nick—so much so that visitors to PIMCO regularly ask how they are doing.

The private Gross is not different from the man you will meet in this book; his focus is just different. On the job, he scrounges for extra returns; on the street walking with Sue, the two scramble to retrieve an errant penny on the pavement because it brings good luck. Someone once calculated that it is not worth Bill Gates's time to bend over and pick up a hundred-dollar bill—he makes more per second at his day job. Gross will happily scramble for one red cent for purely non-economic reasons. He is not ashamed to say that he is superstitious.

Gross is candid, and is willing to surrender secrets about himself even when they reveal his failures and foibles. In both his personal and professional life, he confesses error reluctantly but in full. I once asked him how he had met his wife, and with a rueful grin he shared the story. It seems Bill and Sue each had registered with a dating service, but she took a pass on him the first time. Six months later, when he asked again, she had a change of heart and agreed to meet him for a drink. "Persistence pays off," he told me. When he arrived for their date, he realized that he had left his wallet at the office. He tried to hock his watch in the lobby but there were no takers, so he was forced to ask Sue to pick up the tab. She did, proving herself to be a pretty shrewd investor.

The private Gross is currently white-knuckling Nick through driving lessons; the boy is 15 and in California that means he can get a license on his next birthday. Bill says he has laid down the law: "It will be nice when he can drive himself, I guess," he told me, "as long as he drives himself safely, which is problematic. I'm giving him severe admonitions; if he ever gets a ticket, it's lights out as far as driving is concerned."

But mostly the private Gross putters about his 10,000-square-foot oceanfront home near PIMCO's headquarters, amid his books of history and philosophy and geopolitics, and his stamp collection, and more than a dozen paintings Sue began to produce after she decided modern art is something you *can* do at home. She is so prolific, her husband says, "We're going to have to buy a bigger house."

But this book delves into Bill Gross's Bond King persona. In reading it, we have the benefit of Gross's own hard-earned experience. Yet, more importantly, within these pages Gross's hedgehog view of the investment marketplace unfolds, revealing a perspective and outlook that will help readers prepare for the future.

Acknowledgments

Business has this in common with sports: There is a score and you know who the winners are. Bill Gross is the Babe Ruth of bonds, and I am grateful he agreed to cooperate when I proposed this book to him. He also asked his partners and employees to fill me in on PIMCO's way of managing money; the point man who coordinated these contacts was Mark Porterfield, PIMCO's director of public relations. The amount of work these two men and their associates did to help me is considerable, and I am thankful. If there are inaccuracies in these pages, they are despite PIMCO's best educational efforts.

My literary agent, Esmond Harmsworth, and my editor at John Wiley & Sons, Jeanne Glasser, became my collaborators on this book, patiently helping me transform my first draft into this much more complete and readable version. A first book—and this is mine—is far more punishing on the publisher than the author, and I am grateful to Esmond and Jeanne for leading me up the learning curve.

In writing about financial markets, and especially their history, I am indebted to Richard Smitten, Jesse Livermore's biographer, and to the biographers of Bernard Baruch and J. Pierpont Morgan. I have also exploited information from *The Economist* newspaper as well as the Morningstar Inc., Bloomberg, and ETFConnect.com databases.

I received an enormous amount of support from my editors at MSN Money, notably Mark Palowsky, Richard Jenkins, Erle Norton, and Jon Markman, the best team of bosses I have been fortunate enough to work for. At CNBC I have been aided by colleagues Matt Greco and Mark Haines. More indirectly but no less importantly, I have been fortunate to benefit from a circle of fellow financial journalists without whose help I would not even have wound up in this wing of financial writing: Andy Gluck, Dan Akst, Dan Wiener, Jim Lowell, Rick Green, Mike McDermott, and Randy Myers.

My principal career guidance counselor has been my wife, Joyce Rhea Middleton, who happens to be a school principal. I have been a lucky man, and the best luck I ever had was finding and marrying her. She wrung this book out of me. Our three children, Brendan, Michael, and Margaret, who all are writing books themselves, indulged my absence from more than one important family affair because I was working on this one.

My late mother, Freda, and my dad, George, filled our home with books; it made me long to add one of my own to the shelf. Zane Gray was my mother's favorite author. She liked his Westerns. I like his fishing stories. My dad taught me to fish.

Short Hills, New Jersey
November, 2003

PART ONE

Gross the Man

Introduction

Bill Gross's Day

You would never know from looking at him that William Hunt Gross is one of the richest and most powerful men in the United States. At his trading turret, he sits ramrod straight, his sandy brown hair brushed from front to side, his loose tie wrapped around his shirt collar, gazing at his computer screens in seeming immobility. His workplace is one cubicle among many—albeit the most spacious one—on the crowded, 4,200-square-foot trading floor of Pacific Investment Management Company, or PIMCO. It is on the third floor of a small office building three thousand miles from Wall Street, tucked among palm trees between the Newport Beach Country Club and a mall called Fashion Island, an hour south of Los Angeles—a modest setting, indeed, for the tenth most powerful person in the business world, according to *Fortune* magazine's 2003 poll.

Gross's silence and modesty are part of his legend. He is the object of study and fascination, even of divination: like the water diviners of old who would "read" fields and hills to locate aquifers, bond experts parse his every remark and interpret his gestures to predict future movements in the credit markets. They are so intrigued with Gross and his colleagues that they do not even bother to refer to them by name; instead, they call Gross's bond trading office "The Beach," in honor of the sunny California sands near the PIMCO office.

In the same way that investors analyze legendary investor Warren Buffett's stock trades in excruciating detail, so that if he even takes the slightest interest in a company, the stock spikes, wild guesses and rumors about "what The Beach is doing" run rampant through the relatively tame world of the credit markets. Given Gross's uncanny ability to predict future trends in the economy and his power to move markets for stocks as well as bonds, it is no wonder "The Street" spends so much time trying to outguess "The Beach." Forget the experts who divine decisions made in cryptic meetings of the Federal Reserve, forget the Buffett-ologists who hazard a guess on his latest acquisitions: the real action is in trying to anticipate, interpret, and explain the stream of thoughts coursing through Bill Gross's brain.

Some people are simply smarter than other people, and Gross belongs to the former tribe. In March 2002, Gross's Investment Outlook newsletter was devoted to what he considered glaring inconsistencies in the financial statements of General Electric Company. This most-admired of American corporations—its sterling success usually credited to its razor-sharp management and its relentless ability to boost earnings—was, Gross argued, a flawed version of Warren Buffett's Berkshire Hathaway. Gross described GE not as it is usually known—as an industrial conglomerate—but instead as a ragtag bunch of investments owned by a pool of capital desperately and heedlessly searching for profit opportunities. Unlike Berkshire, which is insulated from outside investors and controlled by a genius, GE's cash-producing arm, GE Capital, is a part of a public corporation that raises money through the sale of commercial paper to institutions like PIMCO. And, despite GE Capital's Triple-A credit rating, Gross wrote, "They nonetheless have commercial paper outstanding which totals three times the size of their bank lines (of credit) which back them up."

Gross was pointing out that GE's structure looked like a tottering tower that was about to fall from the pressure of its enormous debt. GE's cash was as leveraged as a hedge fund, and it was using that cash to buy numerous business, but it lacked someone to select those acquisitions with the skill and care of a Buffett. To top it off, the stock was marketed as if it were one of the safest, gilt-edged blue chips. PIMCO, Gross said, would own no GE commercial paper for "the foreseeable future."

GE and a tide of brokerage firm analysts attacked Gross's analysis vehemently; Gross had not anticipated such an uproar. But GE's paper, including its bonds, sold off immediately. In reaction, GE announced a substantial deleveraging of its borrowings. Experts across the world saw the truth of Gross's analysis: the blue chip to end all blue chips was partly a risky venture fund, with no Warren Buffett or John Doerr at the helm. The prophet of the credit markets had struck with pinpoint accuracy.

Gross's fearless eye has done more than affect single—if dominant—companies; he has been known to move markets, too. On the last day of February, 2000, news of a series of bond purchases, supposedly coming from "The Beach," rocketed through the trading floors of firms like Merrill Lynch, Goldman Sachs, Bear Stearns, and Lehman Brothers. The story was: Gross is out there in the credit markets, and he's buying! Like wildfire, PIMCO's competitors began snapping up Treasuries, good quality corporates, and mortgage bonds. Within hours the price of these bond issues hit the roof and the nation's long-term interest rates tumbled (bond yields are the reciprocal of their price, so when prices rise, rates fall). The fall in rates rattled the nerves of those who believed stocks were dangerously overpriced. A few days later, in March, the stock market hit a high that it has never reached again and began its sickening tumble to who-knows-where.

It was as if everyone began simultaneously wondering whether Bill Gross knew something about the equity markets they did not. Anxious investors, spooked by the clairvoyance of "The Beach," questioned whether the wild returns of the 1990s were a bubble after all and, selling their internet stocks en masse, stampeded like a herd of sheep into the haven of bonds. That day, and in the weeks and months that followed, Gross had more influence over the stock and bond markets than Warren Buffett, President Clinton, or even Alan Greenspan. Is it any wonder that people spend their days and nights interpreting, second-guessing, and analyzing the actions of The Beach?

* * *

Seemingly unaware that the eyes of the financial world are so fixed upon him, Bill Gross adheres to a common daily ritual. His routine is as fixed as a stalagmite.

Gross begins his days with an early 10-minute commute in a Mercedes that could qualify for the Monaco Grand Prix. Fast, hot cars are an obsession with him (although he is a careful, sensible driver). Depending on his mood, he either listens to classical music or to rock (his love for Mozart is matched by a yen for classics of the 1970s like the Doobie Brothers and contemporary artists like the Dave Matthews Band). He follows East Coast business hours, and for a man working in Newport Beach, that means a 5:30 A.M. start at the office. This may seem onerous to some, but to Gross, the California lifestyle is something that can never be compromised.

Once he arrives at The Beach, Gross goes straight to his office. His shirt is starched but the collar is open, the tie draped like vestments, his jacket on a hanger. He flips on his computer screens in the same order and adjusts the pair of fluffy dice in front of him precisely; they display the numbers five and six, the roll at craps when nearly everybody wins. Like a dedicated gambler, he sticks to this routine superstitiously; even the smallest change could cause his luck to turn.

Gross keeps his crowded, busy office funereally quiet, because he hates distractions. (Sometimes he drives his colleagues nuts: "He doesn't say anything for hours!" one of them confided to me.) He sits rigidly like a beanpole praying mantis, his thin form directed in intense thought at his computer screens. Occasionally, when the numbers on the Bloombergs change and he thinks something interesting is happening, his head pivots between the screens as if on ball bearings, like a gun on a battleship. He sits like that behind his trading turret, staring at one screen like a marble statue and then, suddenly, swiveling to face the next.

At 9 A.M.—lunchtime in Manhattan—he walks across the street to the Marriott for his daily exercise, supervised by a tough personal trainer who is a former Marine. Gross habitually works out for an hour and a half each day. His regimen combines an element of cardiovascular exercise with intense yoga and stretching. He cannot still fit into his college chinos, but middle age has taken his waist only to about 35 inches from 32.

At noon he strolls into the daily investment committee meeting, one attraction of which, he admits with a miser's glee, is a free lunch. He leaves the office a little after 4 P.M.—this is the West Coast, remember, and the bond market has been dark for hours—and hits a bucket of balls at his country club. Then he drives back to his home on the ocean in Laguna Beach.

A night out with his wife Sue might include a 5:30 P.M. table at a Mexican restaurant with a total tab of $20; he is back home by 6:30. He collects stamps and reads voraciously—Virginia Woolf got more ink than Alan Greenspan in his "Dow 5,000" column—and is early to bed because, as his work requires, he has to be early to rise, flipping on the Bloombergs in his home office before 5 A.M. He eats the same fruit in his cereal at the same time each morning, because Sue says the antioxidants in the fruit are good for his heart; they are about the only richness in his yogic diet. On the weekend he plays a round of golf; he plays with his wife when they manage to get to their place at Indian

Wells, a golf community outside Palm Springs. "From November to May it is one gorgeous spot, not only the high desert but the temperatures and the golf course and all of that," he says. "It's very peaceful living."

It is peaceful in a Grossian way. When Gross plays golf, he is on a mission. He took the game up late in life and considers himself to be early on the learning curve. His handicap is 13 but, says Mark Kiesel, PIMCO's investment-grade corporate bond specialist, a scratch golfer himself, "in a tournament he becomes an 8 real quick." In fact, Gross plays in several tournaments a year. In 2002 at the AT&T National Pro-Am at Pebble Beach, his foursome included Tiger Woods. "I pursue the game with an obsession," he told me, "much like that six-day marathon that I ran 20-plus years ago. I have to say, though, my obsession is making limited progress in terms of improving my game." He never stops trying; shortly after one of my interviews with him he was headed with Bill Thompson, PIMCO's chief executive, to Oregon's Bandon Dunes, a pair of courses 100 feet above the Pacific ranked by Golf Magazine as among the top 100 in the world.

Bill Gross is not your ordinary number cruncher with a math Ph.D., heading up the fixed income department in a bank. His mystique gives him a bully pulpit that can sway the markets with incredible force. He prizes clarity of thinking and concentration and he lives a rich life outside his work. He explores his inner self and makes decisions with a clarity gained through his yoga practice and his obsessive reading. Whenever he makes a mistake, he feels it keenly: after a particularly off day, he has been known to take the stairs rather than the elevator the next morning so that he does not have to see or speak to anyone. Although voraciously competitive and obsessive, he is a very spiritual, questioning person.

———————— ◆ ————————

Gross has earned his laurels through a combination of techniques that share one thing: rigorous, dedicated self-discipline. If you want to learn from him, the first lesson is to do *nothing* by half measures.

In the rest of this book, I discuss in detail the techniques Gross uses in each area of the bond market. But even more important than his strategies is his intense, Grossian philosophy of investing. Unlike most legendary money managers, Gross sees investing as akin to legalized gambling. He believes he has a "system" that can work as well as advanced blackjack card counting works in Las Vegas. And the advantage for Gross is that, in the bond markets, there is no "house" to play against, and no security guards to toss you out of the casino when they realize you are playing a system.

The second lesson Gross gives us is best encapsulated by the old saying: "Know thyself." Make sure you know what you are doing before you get serious about managing your investments. Know what risks you are exposing yourself to and control them. Play the game for the long term. Above all, know what the odds are. The investing game is not filled with innocent widows and orphans; if you are a rube you are going to lose. Therefore, you need to study up.

Today, Gross remains at the helm of PIMCO, which remains at the top of its game. Whatever his thoughts about the future, he remains for the present glued to his discipline with a fixity that is spectral. Indeed, Gross reminds me of what the cosmologist Martin Rees said of his colleagues in his Scribner Lectures at Princeton University, which were published under the title *Our Cosmic Habitat* (Princeton University Press, 2001). Speculating about the origin and fate of the universe does not faze them, although much of their subject is unknown and may ultimately be unknowable. They are, Rees says, "often in error but never in doubt."

Like Warren Buffett, who also still goes to work every day, Gross has achieved his power and success by exploiting rather elementary notions of value, which an ordinary investor can readily learn. Gross also makes heavy use of institutional investing's big guns—Ph.D.'s in mathematics and the computers they control, as well as crack traders. He also has a mastery of the bond universe's exotic financial derivatives. All these weapons enable him to squeeze extra dollars out of virtually every successful investment—and limit losses on the unsuccessful ones. Buffett is somewhat similar, using a strategy unavailable to individual investors: while he acquires some companies outright, Buffett has taken stakes in others in the form of interest-paying convertible preferred stock that is issued only to him. Because of these advantages, it is almost impossible for average investors to beat Gross or Buffett at their own game. However, you can at the very least come close, and that means making tremendous returns on your bond portfolio. You can confidently expect to improve your investment returns if you heed the wisdom he has acquired in a career spanning more than 30 years.

In Part One of the book, I discuss Gross's life and his career success; in Part Two I analyze the Total Return method Gross employs in detail across all sectors of the bond markets. In Part Three of the book, I show you how to use the Gross method to devise a bond investing strategy and significantly increase your returns.

CHAPTER 1

From $200
to Half a Billion

William Hunt Gross was born on April 13, 1944, in Middletown, Ohio, a midsize town in the state's southwest corner, near the Indiana and Kentucky borders. Located in Butler County, Middletown is a small industrial town halfway between the bright lights of Cincinnati and Dayton. Years later, Gross would fondly recall his Middletown summer afternoons swimming in placid little Butler Creek. It seemed so safe and welcoming in contrast with the swirling torrent of the Mississippi River or the bottomless depth of the Pacific Ocean.

The 1940s were a risky time for children; their growing-up didn't seem as assured as it does today. Polio was a serious threat until April, 1954—when Dr. Jonas Salk's pioneering vaccine went into mass testing—and epidemics of scarlet fever were not uncommon. Gross himself nearly died of scarlet fever when he was two years old, landing in the hospital for the first of what became too many times for his liking.

His middle name, Hunt, came from his mother's side of the family. According to family lore, the Hunts were farmers in Manitoba, Canada, migrating south in the 19th century. One branch of the family moved south to Texas. "That was the H.L. Hunt half that struck it rich," Gross says. "Unfortunately, my half went to Minnesota to farm, and, in the case of my mother, later to Ohio." The oil Hunts are perhaps best known for H.L.'s failed attempt to corner the silver market in the late 1970s. It created a national mania in which families sold silver coins and table service—for as much as $25 an ounce—that was later quashed by federal intervention. Though his own connection with that branch of the family is more than a century distant, Gross muses, "Maybe the markets were in my genes as far back as the 19th century."

His father was a sales executive with Armco Steel, the economic backbone of Middletown. The company, now weakened, still has a mill there under its new name, AK Steel. In the good old days, Armco produced diversified metals for various industrial consumers; in the 1940s and 1950s its principal customers were the leaders of the auto industry, located almost due north in Detroit.

When Gross was 10, his father was transferred to San Francisco to open a sales office for Armco designed to serve customers on the West Coast and in Japan. Complete with their German shepherd, the Grosses boarded the California Zephyr in Chicago and, three days later, arrived in the Golden State. Gross discovered his ability to adjust to new circumstances: it was an exciting time. He was dazzled by the freeways, the endless traffic lights, and the varied activities available in the metropolis; San Francisco was as different from a soot-stained Midwestern steel town as a place could get. Aside from his college years and military service in Vietnam, Gross has not left California since.

Tall and lanky, he now stands 6 feet tall and weighs 175 pounds. "Well, 176 today; I just weighed myself a few minutes ago," he said during an interview in August 2003. He was much thinner in high school and played on the varsity basketball team; he had a good set shot. His high school hero was Jerry Lucas, a top college basketball player from Ohio State who eventually turned pro; Gross kept a scrapbook he still thinks he has narrating Jerry Lucas's career. When it came time for college, his parents pressured him to attend Stanford or some other nearby school but, he says: "I had to get away. That was paramount to me. I needed to assert my independence, so the East Coast was all I considered."

He visited Cornell, Princeton, and Duke. His mother considered Princeton a suitable substitute for Stanford, but Duke was already gaining what has become a premiere reputation in college basketball, and it was Duke he chose. "I broke my mother's heart," he confesses, but Duke also offered a scholarship (academic, not athletic), which Princeton did not, and she assented to his desire to settle into central North Carolina.

He did not make the team.

He majored in psychology and minored in Greek—as in Fraternity Row. At the beginning of his senior year, he was dispatched to fetch doughnuts for Phi Kappa Psi's pledge candidates. It was rainy and he was driving too fast; he lost control of his Nash Rambler and smashed into oncoming traffic. He went through the windshield on the passenger's side and the glass sliced off three-quarters of his scalp. In shock and unaware of this, he was stunned when a doctor soon loomed over him and said, "Son, there's nothing I can do for you." Moments later a state trooper walked into the emergency room with Gross's scalp, however, and the doctor was able to help him after all. Gross has been sensitive, and even a bit vain, about his carefully coifed locks ever since.

His injuries were serious, and Gross spent so much of his senior year in the hospital that he resolved never to return if he could help it. Always athletic, he began a workout regimen with what was becoming his characteristic, obsessive rigor. The most obvious instance of this is when, on a dare, he ran from San Francisco to Carmel, California— a distance of 125 miles—in six days. He ran the last five miles with a ruptured kidney which, of course, sent him to the hospital. He also managed to tear up his knees pounding the Southern California pavement, and today his workout consists of a combination of yoga and work on an exercise bike to limit wear on his joints.

While his scalp and his body mended in a North Carolina hospital, Gross picked up a book entitled *Beat the Dealer*, written by a man named Ed Thorpe. It taught a system for counting cards at blackjack. Not unlike the way Goren taught students of bridge to tally the power of their hands, it simplified a seemingly impossible task. Instead of keeping track of individual cards, the system keeps track of three groups. Twos through sixes count as minus one. Sevens through nines are ignored; they count nil. Tens, face cards and aces are plus one. You do not actually count cards; you just know moment by moment whether the count is negative, meaning a lot of low cards have been dealt, or positive, meaning high cards have fallen. Blackjack is also called 21. Aces count as either one or 11, face cards 10, and all others their own number. Players can draw as many cards as they want, although if they go over 21 they are busted. Dealers (who automatically win ties) cannot draw if their cards total 17 points or more. But they can go bust themselves if, for example, they were to have, say, 12 points showing and draw a face card.

It takes a certain mathematical bent as well as concentration and memory to keep track of the odds at blackjack, but Gross had this knack—he has always been good with numbers and can compute quickly in his head, although he has never considered himself a math genius. He spent his hospital time, and plenty of the rest, studying Thorpe's book and testing his abilities with his fraternity mates. Counting cards with a single deck is elementary; sometimes most of the face cards will fall before the game is half done, so the player can draw without going bust more frequently toward the end. Sometimes the opposite is true, but with only 52 cards, 16 of which are face cards and tens, keeping track is not difficult. For this reason, blackjack tables deal cards from a "shoe" containing as many as six decks. Such a shoe holds 96 cards that count as ten points, plus 24 aces, plus 212 others— and not all the cards are played before they are shuffled again. But the

Thorpe system works regardless, Gross insists, though it is painfully rigorous—all those unpleasant and usually untidy drunks around the table, day after day—and inevitably gets you thrown out when security or pit bosses figure out how you are winning so consistently.

The youthful gambler became absorbed in this endeavor and hatched a plan to try his luck as a professional gambler when he graduated. He had enlisted in the Navy—the alternative was to be drafted, most likely into the Army, and Vietnam was already creeping towards the front page—but he did not have to report until October, 1966. In June, he set off for Las Vegas with a kitty of $200 and a head full of numbers, his psychology major already retreating toward a minor, but not unimportant, interest (Gross is interested in human behavior as it affects markets, not individuals). Gross does not deny what his senior partners say of him, which is that he is not a "people person," detests managing staff or the business and is far more comfortable staring raptly and silently at computer screens of numbers, for hours on end.

Gross moved into the Indian Motel for $6 a day (with a few free nickels kicked back for the slots at a local casino), walked the Strip—he had no car anymore—and began to gamble. "My parents told me I would be back in a day and a half," he once told *The New York Times*. He scrounged for meals to conserve his capital and began to develop not only a real skill for Thorpe's system but an aversion to the lifestyle that goes along with it. At first he took breaks just to get away from the hunched men and women who were his fellow players, of a type that can be found in any gambling den on any continent today—except that back then they were wreathed in thicker smoke and smelled more strongly of booze. But he discovered breaks upset his rhythm as well as his concentration. Soon he was playing 16 hours a day, every day. Never since has Gross shirked labor. He impressed his early bosses with his long hours, and today he holds new hires at PIMCO to a merciless regimen of tough assignments, imposing responsibilities, and midnight oil. In just four months of skill and hard work, he had lined his pockets with $10,000 from the gaming tables, which was enough to finance his MBA. All the while he was learning something Duke had not taught him: how to manage money.

After four months in the casino, Gross reported to the Pensacola, Florida, Naval Air Station to fulfill his enlistment and, he hoped, his dream to become a fighter pilot. Like raw recruits then and now, he and his comrades were put into the capable hands of a drill sergeant. With the draft eliminated, fewer Americans endure this ritual today than did those of Gross's generation. The sheer submission that basic training requires would shock self-esteem gurus into intensive care. Especially when his charges aspire to emerge as Navy aviators, the drill sergeant's duty is to humiliate and harass recruits to the breaking point and beyond. A cocky college boy named Bill Gross was so shaken by the experience that it is one of the military moments he remembers most vividly. He spent half the night cleaning his rifle, and failing inspections nonetheless. It took him so long to make up his bunk to the sergeant's specifications that he slept on the floor. He did push-ups and chin-ups and marched and ran obstacle courses, but Marine Sergeant Alfredo Cruz, Gross relates in his book, *Bill Gross on Investing* (John Wiley & Sons, 1997) was never satisfied. "'You'll never fly a jet, Mr. Gross!' he would scream. 'BLIMPS are more your style!'" Gross ended up flying neither.

He discovered, to his dismay, that he did not have the right stuff. He was bright enough, and could calculate mathematical odds in his head faster than Sgt. Cruz could order 20 push-ups, but the myriad details of flying a supersonic aircraft off the deck of a carrier and into combat were simply overwhelming. "I'm more of a conceptual person," he says, "and conceptual pilots are dead pilots." As an investor, Gross is a generalist, leaving the highly detailed task of selecting individual securities to PIMCO's large staff of portfolio managers and analysts. This is called *top-down*, or "macro," as in macroeconomics: the study of the entire economy, or multiple economies, rather than their constituent parts, like industries and regions. This is the main reason that

PIMCO Total Return's great size—of more than $70 billion—is not an impediment to further success. Gross picks areas of the bond market to stress or avoid; he does not pick individual bonds.

The recruit's desire to be a pilot also paled when he was taken on training flights and discovered the romance of the wild blue yonder had been greatly exaggerated. He hated to fly and still does. As chief investment officer of a key subsidiary of a giant German insurance company, he cannot escape some trips abroad, but he foists as many others on his staff as he can. So Ensign Gross went to Vietnam not to fly jets but to conn small boats that took Navy SEALs up jungle rivers on dangerous and secret missions. It was the SEALs who faced danger; as it turned out, the only time Gross's boat came under fire he was not aboard, having overslept.

Returning from overseas, Gross took a paucity of war stories, the GI Bill and his hard-won $10,000 to the University of California at Los Angeles. Investing was in his unshed blood. And no sooner had he embarked on his studies than he found that Ed Thorpe had written a second book, called *Beat the Market*. It preached the virtues of one of Wall Street's most obscure products: convertible bonds (also known as *converts*). These are debt instruments that can, under the right circumstances, be transmuted into equity. Meanwhile they pay a nice dividend. Convertibles have mutated and proliferated ever since—Warren Buffett has often used them to boost his returns—but they remain a highly specialized product, because they require two equally rigorous levels of analysis; the prospects of the issuer's common stock as well as its debt. Thorpe argued that the peculiar difficulties of analyzing convertibles and their relative scarcity made them ripe for exploitation by a crafty investor. Obscurity in an investment product breeds opportunity. Peter Lynch built his reputation on finding companies the rest of the market had overlooked, usually because they were so little-known.

The famous Efficient Markets Theory postulates that small-company stocks will outperform those of big ones in the end, and they do. One of the main reasons cited by theorists is information disparity. The idea is this: so many investors concentrate on the world's largest corporations—like GE, Coca Cola, and General Motors—that the minute "news" breaks out about one of these stocks, the market reacts immediately. People know more about these companies and therefore—according to theorists—they are more fairly valued as their prices react almost instantaneously to new information. Smaller companies are not covered as much by analysts and fewer investors spend their days watching them. Therefore, Efficient Markets theorists consider smaller companies more opaque and unnoticed. As a result, their valuations are less likely to be accurate because they react slowly to information, and since fewer people feel they need them in a core portfolio, they are often undervalued. Thus, Efficients Markets mavens see small caps as more likely to see their market capitalizations grow over the long-term than the best-known mega-corporations.

Similarly, as few investors in the 1970s took much notice of converts, and as at least part of a convert's price is affected by the same kind of information that affects equity prices, theorists would argue that converts were an ideal place for Gross to spot pricing inefficiencies and undervaluations. Today there are a couple of dozen mutual funds that specialize in convertibles, including PIMCO Convertibles Fund, but in 1970 there was only one, and it had so few assets that it was invisible. Gross wrote his master's thesis on converts, and thus quite unwittingly sealed his professional fate.

Young MBAs who went looking for work on Wall Street in 2002 (at the depth of the bear market) can identify with those from 30 years earlier, when the bear was also abroad in the land. Freshly certified as a master of business administration, Gross entered a marketplace that did not need any, particularly on the West Coast, which he preferred for lifestyle reasons, and which was an even more distant cousin of Broad and Wall streets than it is today. He was slumping at the breakfast table one Sunday morning when his mother, who was visiting, did what mothers of such sons often do—read the want ads. She spotted an opening at Pacific Mutual Life Insurance Company for a junior credit analyst. The son obediently applied, although like most young securities analysts before and since he really wanted to work on stocks, not bonds. He never imagined that it would lead to a world-famous career; all he hoped was that it might give him a shot at switching to equities in a year or two.

Gross's preparation for the Pac Mutual job could not have been better. "Here was a guy who wrote his master's thesis on convertible bonds," recalls A. Benjamin Ehlert, who interviewed him for the job and became his supervisor. "That was of great interest to us." An insurance company makes money by investing the premiums it collects, and in those days Pac Mutual invested primarily in bonds, mortgages, and private placements (an institutional variant of a bond). Gross's credentials were excellent and, Ehlert says, he was obviously very smart. He was hired.

<hr/>

It would not take long for Gross to realize he had landed at exactly the right place at exactly the right time. Not long before he was hired, Pac Mutual had retained the consulting firm McKinsey & Co. to advise it on new business opportunities, and the opportunity it recommended was in equity mutual funds. The insurance company had legions of salesmen who could, with a little training, sell funds as well as policies. Pac Mutual had created a subsidiary, Pacific Investment Management Company, to implement this strategy, and it was this entity that Gross quickly joined. In his heart, he hoped—at the time—that a transfer to equities would come his way.

The fact that PIMCO existed before Gross even joined the company may confuse some readers who think he and two partners founded the company. Technically, they did not. Gross and the other two men, James Muzzy and William Podlich, did indeed create the company that PIMCO has become, and in that sense they founded the firm that today has a commanding influence over fixed income investing. A decade later, in 1982, they would begin a process of weaning their investment operation from the insurance parent and formally establishing their independence from it. But in the first decade they inhabited a corporate shell and, bit by bit, simply took it over.

It was not hard. Muzzy, who joined the company at the same time as Gross and who was also a portfolio manager, explains that "after a year and a half they discovered the insurance agents didn't want to get close to mutual funds." Simultaneously, Gross was discovering that his boss, Ehlert, was not averse to the idea of active bond management, and indeed was willing to push the idea forward. With conventional bond management techniques languishing, Pac Mutual's investment committee agreed to fence off a $5 million portion of its bond portfolio for Ehlert to run, and he in turn gave the job to Gross.

The insurance company had little to lose. Massive overspending on the Great Society and the Vietnam War—guns and butter—was leading to accelerating inflation. Today's youngsters who watch reruns of the 1970s television program "The Mary Tyler Moore Show" undoubtedly miss the humor in the opening credits: the lead character picks up a package of meat at the supermarket, grimaces, shrugs and throws it into her cart. Prices of goods went up weekly or monthly in that decade; consumers were continuously shocked and disgusted. President Nixon was imposing price controls—President Ford unveiled "Whip Inflation Now" pins soon thereafter, though neither he nor his successor, Jimmy Carter, did anything to accomplish that goal—but in the bond market there were no controls, and as inflation went up, bond prices went down. Banks embraced the trend with a new product called certificates of deposit, with lush and rising yields. Treasury bonds, in the gallows humor of Wall Street, came to be known as certificates of confiscation. Even though their coupons seem extraordinarily high compared to today (sometimes approaching 20 percent), because of inexorably rising rates, once investors bought them they quickly saw prices fall through the floor. It was like catching a falling knife.

Indefatigable and confident, Gross flourished. He found pennies under rocks. It was still the age of carbon paper, typing pools, and expensive long distance calls, when the most comprehensive data about bonds was published in a newspaper, the Bond Buyer. Michael Bloomberg would not invent his machines tracking the minutiae of bond trading until the next decade. Trading was done on the phone, barking orders to and negotiating fiercely with the New York desks of bond specialist firms like Salomon Brothers and Goldman Sachs. Particular opportunities existed in very thinly traded securities called private placements. These were, and are, paper instruments different from the regular kind only in that they had not been vetted by the Securities & Exchange Commission, and so could be bought and sold only by institutions. In one instance, the voice over the phone in Gross's left hand told him he could buy $2 million worth of a private 7 percent preferred stock of General Telephone & Electric Company for 79, meaning a price of $790 for each $1,000 face amount of the shares. Through the phone in his right hand he offered to sell it, and got a price of 89. Such a trade is called a cross; PIMCO owned the securities only for the instant it took to confirm both deals. In that moment when the right hand knew exactly what the left hand was doing, Gross bagged a profit of more than $200,000. "It was a pretty huge trade involving no risk whatsoever," he noted to me in an interview. "That's the biggest cross I've ever made. If you can cross . . . for 10 points with no risk, you're doing your job."

There was no doubt at the insurance company that it had a rising star on its hands. The then head of Pac Mutual's investments and subsequently its chairman, Walter Gerken, was sufficiently impressed by Gross to take him along to an important meeting of insurance company executives in Williamsburg, Virginia. With their vast portfolios of bonds, insurers were suffering under inflation, and the theme of the meeting was how to cope. Gross was not on the program, but he piped up often enough from the audience to be noticed. Gerken is now retired but maintains an office in the same Newport Beach complex as Gross, and he greeted me one spring afternoon to reminisce about his prodigy. Recalling the investment conference, he chuckled. "A friend of mine came up to me there and said, 'Boy, you've got one smart guy here, Walter.' And I said, 'Keep your cotton-picking hands off!'"

Gerken knew his Boy Wonder was being courted by rival firms, although he might have been surprised had he known that there were only two of them. In the case of the first, Gross traveled up to San Francisco to interview for a job with Claude Rosenberg, whose Rosenberg Capital Management at the time was a much bigger and more prestigious operation than PIMCO. "I would have taken that job if it had been offered," Gross now says, but it was not. Ironically, Rosenberg prided himself on his judgment of talent. He later wrote a book, *Investing With the Best* (John Wiley & Sons, 1986), in which he opined, "Finding the best person or the best organization to invest your money is one of the most important financial decisions you'll ever make." The man Rosenberg picked over Gross never made a name, at least one that Google can find.

Rosenberg did, however, recommend Gross to another firm, which was opening an office in Los Angeles to manage bonds. That firm, which no longer exists, offered to double Gross's salary, which was in the $25,000 range. Gross agonized over the offer for more than two weeks. He desperately wanted the money and the recognition it conveyed, but he realized: "I just wasn't the type of guy to get up and desert a family that had been good to me, so I stayed. That was the last chance I had."

PIMCO was being good to Gross, but he chafed under what he and his colleagues, Muzzy and Podlich, regarded as its complacent paternalism. One of them confided to me that he regarded the insurance company executives as "lifers" who lacked the drive to establish a world-class shop. Promotions did not matter to Gross—Gerken says it was clear he was not "planning to be head of a department; he wanted to manage money"—but his compensation did, and he was not shy about asking for a raise. In one instance enshrined in PIMCO lore, Gross, Muzzy, and Podlich scheduled a meeting with Gerken and demanded big raises—from the $50,000 they were then making to $75,000. Gerken assented, only to discover that instead of being grateful, they began almost immediately to regret that they had not asked for more.

Indeed, the story of PIMCO as an organization is one of a careful and unrelenting effort by Gross, Muzzy, and Podlich to share in the subsidiary's profits and its equity. They did just that, and each became a very rich man. However, with the 30 percent interest in PIMCO it continues to retain, the insurance company is richer still. Allianz AG paid $3.5 billion to acquire 70 percent of PIMCO in 2000. Pacific Life's interest is all the more valuable because it came at such a minuscule cost. "The most they ever had invested in it was two or three years of negative carry—one or two hundred thousand dollars," Podlich estimates. Gross's share of the pie has been reported to be $233 million, plus a $200 million five-year contract, through 2005, in addition to his regular salary and bonuses. Considering his stature in the business, Gross's regular income is probably on the order of $50 million annually. All told, Bill Gross is a half-billion dollar man.

Gross's portfolio was quickly outshining the rest of the insurance company's investments. This prompted Gerken to persuade Southern California Edison Company, whose board of directors overlapped with Pac Mutual's, to let Gross manage a portion of the utility's bonds. The power company gave him $10 million in 1973 and it was from this point, when he had a paying customer, that Gross dates the start of his investment record, which has since compounded at an average rate of 10.11 percent annually. Despite accelerating inflation, his performance surged; he racked up back-to-back gains in 1975 and 1976 of nearly 18 percent. Once again, because some of Pac Mutual's directors sat on the boards of the best of the blue chips, Gross's and Gerken's feats came to the attention of American Telephone & Telegraph Company in New York. In 1977, PIMCO inked what was then the most important deal of its life, becoming the first West Coast investment firm to run money for one of the world's largest corporations, the first non-bank to manage a portion of its bonds, and the first specialty fixed-income management firm it ever hired.

In the 1970s, Gross was a pioneer in using unconventional bonds to diversify the standard holdings of governments and gilt-edged corporates. Convertibles, of course, had always been at home in his portfolios, but he also added mortgage pass-throughs, which today account for a third of the total market. He embraced derivatives, like Treasury options, and emerging markets debt. All of these offer what bond investors call "carry," meaning a premium over less-risky alternatives. Gross became adept, and ultimately the world leader, in maximizing carry in a portfolio while keeping risk to acceptable levels. Rather like stock investors who try to buy undervalued stocks with high "beta," the measurement of a stock's potential to appreciate that is unrelated to the entire market's potential to appreciate, Gross attempted to find bonds that had a carry that was disproportionate to the risks involved in holding them. He was not just looking for bonds that were "cheap" compared to the market. Instead, he selected bonds that were cheap (that is, bonds with a high carry) related to their own fundamentals.

The very highest-yielding bonds, like below-investment-grade (junk) bonds, have a lot of carry, but most of it signifies added risk. Gross managed to squeeze carry out of Treasury bond derivatives, securities that were mathematically related to but not as safe as Grandma's old T-bills. Here he found quirks in pricing: carry that at times was vastly disproportional to the risks involved in the derivative structure (U.S. Treasuries by themselves are considered to have "no" risk, because the risk of a U.S. government default is so remote as to be considered negligible by experts—if it occurred, it would cause a meltdown of the world financial system).

Gross's skill and cunning quickly set him apart from the insurance company investment team. Muzzy quickly became his partner, his colleague as an investor, and his friend. The two of them became the prime salesmen for the emerging PIMCO concept of total return bond investing. Ehlert helped. "Bill and I looked so young, people thought we were too young to entrust" with their money, Muzzy says.

"Ben was the guy with the seasoning; he brought a little credibility when he walked into a meeting."

As eager as Gross was in his early years to promote PIMCO, flying (despite his fear) to sales calls far and wide, he did not like glad-handing clients. He also did not like that it distracted him from his work. The young portfolio manager had begun reading *Reminiscences of a Stock Operator* (John Wiley & Sons, 1993, originally published in 1923), the fabulous and fictionalized biography of Jesse Livermore, the most successful stock operator of the 1920s. Livermore was a shrewd student of markets and their psychology. He made and lost eight fortunes—he killed himself the last time—and he relates in the book that he always brought ruin on himself by failing to follow his own well-tested rules. The most basic of these is to know yourself. In his office, Gross has a picture of Livermore in high dandy, from top hat to spats, with this quote: "In actual practice, an investor has to guard against many things, and most of all against himself."

Fortunately, Muzzy not only did not mind the meeting-and-greeting of potential clients, he enjoyed it. He and Gross complemented rather than competed against each other. Muzzy was gregarious and outgoing, Gross shy and introverted. Muzzy got along easily with people as the firm grew, including subordinates, whereas Gross was clumsy and distant. Muzzy enjoyed explaining in great detail exactly what PIMCO—Gross—did and how it—he—did it; Gross would much rather actually be doing it. Neither, however, much enjoyed the management aspects of running an investment boutique. As they say, every business is different but the management issues—costs, hiring and firing, and so on—of an investment company are not all that different from those of a lemonade stand.

Help came in the form of the firm's third founder, William Podlich. He had joined Pac Mutual five years before the other two and, when Walter Gerken was recruited from Northwestern Mutual a few years later to head the insurance company's investments, he named Podlich his assistant. When Gerken moved up to become chief

executive of the insurance company, Podlich remained in his lieu-
tenant's role to the incoming investment boss, Ott Thompson. By the
time Muzzy and Gross were nudging PIMCO in a new direction,
Podlich was handling the investment operation's consolidated record-
keeping, administration, and planning—in short, the business. As they
worked together and began to talk about transforming what was
effectively Pac Mutual's back pocket into the sharpest investment
company in the fixed income industry, they realized they could function together as what all three refer to as a "three-legged stool."

Muzzy explains: "Most firms are run by the investment department guys. They get sucked into the business issues, and they lose
focus on running the money, and performance goes or they shut the
doors and don't accept new business." So PIMCO would be different.
Gross would run the money, Muzzy would run client relations, and
Podlich would run the company. Podlich continued in that role into
the early 1990s, finally surrendering it to the firm's current chief executive, William Thompson.

The three-legged stool has continued as PIMCO's business model.
Investment managers, who work for Gross, have counterparts called
account managers, who work for Muzzy. The account teams are fully
qualified to run portfolios, and switching between the two sides is not
without precedent: Paul McCulley, now a partner and PIMCO's chief
Fed watcher, was originally hired as an account manager. But the
account teams are the people who interface with the firm's institutional clients. About 80 of the Fortune 100 companies have PIMCO
accounts, and when they want to know about their money, they call
account rather than portfolio managers. Meanwhile a relatively small
team works directly for Thompson, hiring and firing, writing checks,
and planning the firm's future. The three men are still the team's ultimate partners, holding each other to account with the same zeal they
demand of their subordinates. Gross "will look over my shoulder at
times, and I've done that with him if I felt he's done something I did-
n't like," Thompson says. "On the business side he can act as a pretty

damn good conscience for me—like, 'Get costs down over there!' He's got a great business mind, but he allows others, including myself, to pull our weight on the business side, and it doesn't dilute his effort and his thinking."

Back in 1974, meanwhile, Congress passed the Employee Retirement Income Security Act, or ERISA; this made it a responsibility of the Department of Labor to ensure that pension fund managers disinterestedly function as fiduciaries. The fiduciary would act as the fictive "prudent man" of finance. The policy idea was this: Congress believed companies who managed their own pension funds were wracked by conflicts of interest. Rather than act as fiduciaries for their current and future retirees, they acted to benefit themselves, owning large blocks of company stock and sometimes trading in it to satisfy management's short-term needs. ERISA was designed to encourage companies to use outside managers to supervise their pension funds, and for companies to give those managers an unprecedented level of independence.

Suddenly, it was a great time to be a completely independent fixed-income management company. PIMCO continued to beat its rivals handily. The company could sell itself as an independent, leading firm in the management of bonds, which were then the main class of securities used in pension fund investment. Ehlert recalls that when he retired from Pacific Life (the firm ultimately demutualized) in 1981, PIMCO's assets totaled $2 billion. When PIMCO hired him in 1984 as a consultant, they were $6 billion. "That's pretty impressive, to triple assets under management in three years," he says.

During Ehlert's absence, a pivotal event had occurred: PIMCO had won independence from the insurance company. Tensions between the dynamic investment side and the staid insurance side had been rising for years. A. Michael Lipper, founder of the eponymous mutual fund analysis company, says the emblem of this gulf is what he calls "the parking lot problem." The head of the insurance company pulls into his parking spot each day in a Buick. The head of the investment unit pulls up in a Ferrari. Compensation in seven figures is rare among insurers; among investment managers it is common.

By 1981, Podlich says, "It became pretty obvious that a choice people in PIMCO had was to leave." Investment professionals wanted a share of the relatively huge profits they were bringing in. Podlich was still working for Ott Thompson as an executive of the insurance company when the two men studied the matter. "As we started to think about spinning it off, Ott thought I should go with it to help manage it," Podlich says. "That was okay with me. I could see the growth potential better than the insurance company could. Of course, at that time no one dreamed of what ultimately the size of PIMCO would become."

Thompson and his boss, Gerken, independently polled other firms for advice, as well. Gerken consulted Robert A. Day, founder and chairman of Trust Company of the West (TCW), which had gotten its start a decade before. "He had a conversation with Walter about the facts of the management business," Podlich says. "Day said if you don't act, you're going to lose those guys." TCW today is an $85 billion investment management firm handling equities as well as fixed income securities and is, like PIMCO, owned by a European firm (in this instance, Société Générale SA).

In 1982, therefore, Pac Life entered into an agreement with Gross, Muzzy, and Podlich that gave them a share of the profits their operation generated. Also about this time, the outward, physical signs of PIMCO's corporate culture were taking shape. The partners consulted Peter Druker, the great maven of organizational structure, who recommended they adopt a flat, non-heirarchical structure. PIMCO does not have any corner offices. Gross's own, off one side of the trading floor, would humiliate a bank vice president. It is scarely large enough for visitors' chairs. If someone needs to take notes, a panel about the size of an ink blotter slides out of Gross's desk. If a visiting potentate drops by—Bill Ford once landed his yacht at Newport Beach to discuss his company's bonds with Gross—his retinue has to wait in the hall.

During the 1990s, the emerging organization remained a relatively unknown firm outside the world of pension managers and other institutional investors. Gross's monthly portfolio musings, called "Investment Outlook" (which now can be viewed at the company's web site *www. pimco.com*), were sent to the firm's clients but attracted little public interest. The firm took no interest in public mutual funds until 1987, when it launched PIMCO Total Return, and indeed has since been slow to create them; most of the municipal-bond portfolios were created in the late 1990s, long after firms like John Nuveen & Co., Fidelity Investments, and Vanguard Group had made them familiar to investors. Gross did have a high profile among connoisseurs of the market. He appeared once on Louis Rukeyser's "Wall Street Week" sporting a haircut like Sonny Bono's, with Peter Lynch beside him on the couch. But the great bull market in stocks during the 1980s and the 1990s eclipsed bonds in the public imagination, and Gross's public profile was low.

(Today a number of public mutual funds are marketed under PIMCO's name, including a host of equity funds, but none except the bond portfolios are managed at The Beach. They are subadvised through other subsidiaries of Allianz. PIMCO Advisors Distributors, which wholesales all of them to brokerage firms and their customers, is headquartered in Connecticut.)

The obscure years were wonderful for Gross's investors, however. In 1981, when yields on long Treasury bonds were $15\frac{1}{2}$ percent, Paul Volcker yielded to inflation hawks and began the arduous process of bringing down interest rates. Over the following two decades, the Federal Reserve slashed rates by two-thirds. Bond prices rose correspondingly, raining down capital gains as well as coupons on bondholders, with PIMCO Total Return steadily beating the market—the Lehman Brothers Aggregate Bond Index—by between 0.5 percent and 1.5 percent per year. Even as rates declined into single digits in the 1990s, Gross's fund delivered double-digit gains to its shareholders in five of the 10 years between 1993 and 2002. In the 1980s and

1990s, anyone working in the credit markets considered Gross a legend in his own time.

By the early 1990s, Podlich was yearning to step back from PIMCO and become more active in Orange County and California politics, where he remains an important member of the Democratic Party. The firm recruited Bill Thompson as CEO to help lead what it viewed as its next growth step—formal independence from the insurance company as a publicly traded company. A long-time friend and ally of Gross, William Cvengros, who was a senior executive of the insurance company, assumed the role of chairman of the resulting company, PIMCO Advisors. It was PIMCO Advisors that began promoting PIMCO's portfolios as public mutual funds. PIMCO Advisors was 35 percent owned by the insurance company, 25 percent by PIMCO's partners, and the balance by the public. It was also this company that was transformed in 2000 into a subsidiary of Allianz AG, with the German insurer owning 70 percent and Pac Life 30 percent.

———◆———

The deal transformed PIMCO into an autonomous subsidiary of Allianz, its corporate culture intact. The Beach overlooks its namesake, just beyond a golf course and across the Pacific Coast Highway, with Santa Catalina and some drilling platforms sparkling 26 miles out into the Pacific. This view is ignored, however, in favor of a forest of Bloombergs and a giant TV monitor on the wall (silently) broadcasting CNBC. Gross demands of his people the same kind of dedication, long hours, and loyalty that he has invested himself. PIMCO is as quiet as an ant colony, but just as busy; a new employee's first years are a period of hazing of which Sgt. Cruz would approve. "It's almost like the first year at West Point, and I did the first year at West Point," says Mark Kiesel, PIMCO's investment-grade corporate bond specialist, who joined the firm in 1996. "It's not fun." But the point is the same one Sgt. Cruz had, to separate those who belong from those who do not. Those who work out are, as human resources consultants say, incentivized. Teams of first-year employees compete for cash prizes, handed out at the end of the Secular Forum (described in Chapter Four), which range up to $35,000. Pay and performance bonuses make early millionaires of the best. PIMCO's most senior managers, its managing directors—whom Gross calls partners—share in the firm's profits and in an equity interest in the company, even under the Allianz umbrella. They also share both profits and equity with junior partners and executive vice presidents. "You have to equitize the second and third generations," Muzzy says.

Gross emerged from the Allianz deal rich as Croesus, which makes him, like other plutocrats, a social magnet. He hates it. "A cocktail party is my idea of the worst example of wasted time I could imagine anybody spending," he says. His assistant, Danelle Reimer, goes through multiple invitations every day, many of them from charities. "A lot of them are very heart-warming and valid," Gross says. "I take them home, but I don't go out and sip a few bottles of wine and be feted." In one of his "Investment Outlook" columns, he called torture that annual glut of obligatory parties that precedes Christmas. In another, he reported a visit he and wife Sue made to the home of Microsoft founder Bill Gates for cocktails, chatter, and then a check to the charity that was the beneficiary of the evening's entertainment. Gross was so nervous that when he was introduced to Gates he called him Mike. America's No. 2 business leader only grinned at America's No. 10 (their respective Fortune rankings) and handed him off to his wife, and so, miserable and embarrassed, he proceeded down the receiving line.

Since he cannot ignore parties altogether, he hosts them—sparingly. He told me, "What I like to do is every 10 years or so throw a big bash." In the summer of 2003, he chartered a luxury cruise ship to sail his family, his PIMCO colleagues, and 100 Orange County Teachers of the Year to Alaska's fjords for more than a week. "That's my idea of a party, and I try to keep that to once every 10 or 20 years."

Gross's spirituality has never led him to organized religion, but rather towards life around him. His wife and son are Roman Catholic—

his father was, too, but not his mother—and he attends Mass, but he does not take communion and his musings during the homily are mostly his own. A *Newsweek* magazine article about yoga quoted him as describing it as "physical training, not something spiritual or religious." But Eastern religions, notably Buddhism, are "quite apropos to my own thinking," he told me. "They tend to focus on the present moment, the need to look inward and to focus on your inner soul, as opposed to outer salvation.... Their belief is that God is in each and every living thing, and our task is to find it, whether through meditation or contemplation or living and (performing) service within the community."

Befitting a man of his wealth and influence, Gross is active in philanthropy: Bill's charitable works are directed primarily toward the community of Newport Beach and surrounding Orange County. When Allianz, the current corporate owner, acquired PIMCO, Gross and his partners established a $10 million foundation that focuses on Orange County communities. Gross and his family have a private foundation as well, called the Gross Family Foundation. Most of Gross's philanthropy is directed at education: when his son Nick began attending Sage Hill School in Newport Beach, his father funded a scholarship program intended to bring minority enrollment in the private prep school up to 15 percent. For 11 years, their foundation has underwritten annual cash awards totaling $120,000 to Orange County's 50 Teachers of the Year. "It goes straight to the teacher; they can buy a car. In many cases, they buy supplies for their classes, which is touching beyond belief," he says.

The Gross Family Foundation is small but, its founder told me, "I suspect that five years from now... it will rank in the top 50 of all private foundations in the United States, in terms of assets." That would, according to The Foundation Center, mean it would be endowed with at least $865 million. "It won't be the Gates Foundation," Gross told me, "with tens of billions, but it will have the same fairly broadly based responsibility to disseminate wealth in a productive fashion. That will keep me and Sue and hopefully the kids busy for generations to come. I look forward first of all to making the money to fund that foundation, and secondly I look forward to making sure the funds go out. Not in the right direction—there are a lot of right directions—but to make sure it's meaningful in terms of giving back to the community."

PIMCO's emergence onto the public stage, which began in 1987 and has reached a crescendo today, has amplified Bill Gross's thin, reedy voice but has not muted his willingness to stake out controversial positions. He supported Reaganomics from the outset, predicting in September 1981 that it would spell the end of the bear market in stocks, which actually occurred the following August. A few months later, in October, he predicted a bull market in bonds, which indeed assumed historic proportions as long interest rates began their 20-year decline from 15$\frac{1}{2}$ percent. He challenged the New Economy thesis in October of 1999, arguing that technologies like the Internet were actually far more beneficial to consumers than companies. "Stockholders beware," he wrote. "The consumer via the Net may turn out to be your worst enemy instead of your best friend." The following month, he likened Internet stocks to a Ponzi scheme. Just four months later technology stocks began to melt down.

He attracted perhaps the most attention of his entire career in September 2002 with an "Investment Outlook" headlined "Dow 5,000." Gross's bearishness toward stocks has characterized him throughout his working life. He simply does not buy the prevailing wisdom that stocks always beat bonds. There are too many exceptions to this general rule, he argues, the most glaring being that investment results are determined by where you begin as well as by where you end. He has written on the subject endlessly. His April, 2001, "Investment Outlook" was headlined "Ticker Tape Charade." But when he declared that "stocks stink" in September, he elicited the wrath of the whole stock-centric universe. The online magazine *Slate*, published like my mutual funds column by Microsoft's MSN network, sneered at Gross in these words: "The proclamation was a little like a teetotaler proclaiming this year's Beaujolais Nouveau undrinkable. Someone who never touches the stuff should not have much credibility as a critic." It accused him of "talking his book," or promoting his own investments over those of his rivals. "His job is to think that stocks are damaged goods," the *Slate* article opined.

Gross was surprised by the vehemence of his critics, but then, he always is. In March, 2003, the avowed Republican and Vietnam veteran used his bully pulpit to lament the Iraq War. "Preemptive attacks? Kill them before they kill us?" he wrote. "I am heartbroken that it has come to this and I fear for my country's proud heritage and, even more, for its future." *The Wall Street Journal* took him to task, and in its news, rather than its editorial, columns, in a report headlined, "Pimco's Chief Says His Controversial Peace." One of the Wall Street figures quoted in the article labeled Gross's remarks "a feel-good piece from someone who lives in California, which isn't a particularly risky place."

Actually, Gross favors the Left Coast for its weather and golf, not its politics, although he is the kind of fiscal conservative and social liberal his party's right wing loathes. And while some may question his political judgment, that is not what has made him famous. As I explain in the next chapter, it is his complex philosophy of investing and his canny eye that makes Wall Street sit up and take notice when Bill Gross announces his thoughts on just about any topic under the sun.

CHAPTER 2

Total Return Investing

Bonds have never been the sexiest category of investments. Instead, people have considered them safe, conservative, old-ladyish, the most boring investing category, and the one least likely—especially alongside risky hedge funds and common stocks—to attract glamour or attention. More than anyone, Bill Gross has changed that image; but even he found it hard to achieve much recognition until recently. Outside the sprawling marketplace for bonds, his long career went largely unnoticed until the past few years.

The only other name that might appear in the same sentence as Buffett used to be Peter Lynch, who as pilot of the Fidelity Magellan Fund between 1977 and 1990 racked up a jaw-dropping cumulative gain of 2,500 percent. (And Lynch was not even the best manager that fund ever had; Fidelity founder Edward C. Johnson III, who ran it from 1963 to 1972, did even better.) In 1997, when Gross published his first and only book, *Everything You've Heard About Investing is Wrong!,* his publisher, Random House, felt constrained to label him on the cover "The Peter Lynch of bonds."

Within two years of the publication of Gross's book (which was subsequently issued again by John Wiley & Sons as *Bill Gross on Investing*), *Barron's* magazine was proclaiming Gross the Baron of Bonds for his consistently superior results. Increasingly, financial journalists were turning to Gross to explain bonds, the fixed-income market and the Federal Reserve, which ultimately calls the cadence to fixed income's march. He was so sought after—and, being unabashed in admitting he loved the publicity, so available—that PIMCO built a television studio for him at its headquarters. (When he appears on CNBC these days, that is where he is sitting, across the continent from the television station, with extra ties, a jacket, and a small TV makeup kit just out of camera range. On the job, he does not tie his ties or wear a jacket—or sport pancake makeup, for that matter.) His partners were aghast at the cost, but PIMCO saved the hours Gross was schlepping to a hired studio in Pasadena, and Gross's time is PIMCO's money, including those partners' share of the profits.

In 2000, the mutual fund analysis firm, Morningstar Inc., named Gross its Fixed-Income Manager of the Year. It was the second time he achieved that distinction, which made him the only two-time winner of this acknowledgement. In announcing its decision, Morningstar took particular note of Gross's decision to buy Treasuries, which racked up big gains that year as the government, still awash in surpluses at the time, announced plans to buy them back, increasing their scarcity. Morningstar said in announcing the honor that, among the nation's bond managers that year, "no one really came close" to Gross's adroit steps, which also included bulking up on mortgages and slashing corporate bonds, which were beginning a three-year slide.

Morningstar was recognizing Gross in his role at the helm of PIMCO Total Return Fund, which he manages in addition to performing his chief investment officer duties. Total Return is the nation's largest actively managed mutual fund, with assets of $72.2 billion. PIMCO Total Return is also the best-performing fund of its type since its inception in 1987. Morningstar's data for the 15-year period

Table 2.1   Gross and the Competition

Fund	Annualized performance in %, 1988–2003
PIMCO Total Return	9.23
Vanguard Total Bond Index	8.05
Fidelity Intermediate Bond	7.55
Lehman Bros. Aggregate	8.35

Notes: 15 years ended July 31, 2003; selected funds with more than $1 billion of assets
Source: Morningstar Inc.

ended July 31, 2003, shows the fund beating all of its rivals handily, and trouncing the standard industry measure, the Lehman Brothers Aggregate Bond Index, by 0.88 percent.

When Gross's record is adjusted for the 14 years before he began managing a public fund, it is even better: annualized returns of 10.11 percent, fully a point above his benchmark.

The bear market saw the most glamorous and largest fund of the 1990s—Vanguard 500 Index—turn to dust, shedding more than 9 percent of its value in 2000, 12 percent the next year, and 22-plus percent the year after that. Owning all the nation's largest, fastest-growing companies went from being a no-brainer to being brain dead. Suddenly a smart investor who did not just track his marketplace, but beat it, began to look intelligent indeed, especially since his marketplace was cooking. In 2002, *Fortune* magazine promoted Gross to Bond King.

Now Gross was in the big leagues, at least in the public's perception; he had been there more than two decades in the eyes of his peers. When *Fortune* in 2003 ranked what it called "the 25 most powerful people in business," only two were professional investors: Gross, who was slotted No. 10, and Buffett, who was No. 1.

This level of outperformance—substantially ahead of the market average, by between 0.50 and 1.00 percentage points, but not more—is what PIMCO has always said it tries to attain. Gross's investment philosophy is to use a variety of strategies to eke out small incremental increases in bond returns rather than to take daredevil risks. Using one of the metaphors that creep into nearly every paragraph he utters (one of the reasons he is so easily understood by journalists and other laymen), he likens what he does to hitting frequent singles and doubles, as opposed to much rarer home runs.

In baseball, home run hitters tend to strike out a lot, and in 2000 the stock market, which had been batting 1,000, struck out spectacularly, beginning a three-year decline that eventually would take the high-flying Nasdaq down 70 percent. Whereas PIMCO Total Return's single-digit gains had looked embarrassingly modest in 1999, when the average high-technology stock fund soared 129 percent, they began to look sparkling as tech stocks tumbled into the abyss. The fund advanced 8.45 percent in 2000, when tech funds were falling 31.7 percent. It gained another 7.54 percent in 2001, when tech's decline accelerated to a loss of 36.3 percent. It added 8.77 percent more to its shareholders' pockets in 2002, when the tech slide took once-glamorous funds down an astonishing 42.7 percent.

Gross and Buffett have a history, albeit an incredibly tiny one. When Gross was early in his career, Buffett "came by and borrowed some money from me," he jokes. Actually, Buffett and his partner, Charley Munger, came to Pacific Mutual Life, where Gross was a junior credit analyst, seeking to borrow $10 million. At the time, in the early 1970s, Berkshire Hathaway was relatively unknown. "It consisted of Sees Candy and S&H Green Stamps and a sort of dilapidated industrial complex in the Northwest," Gross recalls. Buffett wanted to arrange a private placement in order to acquire a small insurance company called GEICO. Gross was part of the team that analyzed Berkshire Hathaway's books, and recommended the insurance company do the deal. It did and, Gross says, "I haven't seen him since." Of course, since implementing his strategy of using insurance-company cash flows to fund his investments, Buffett has needed to borrow less and less.

In the intervening years, Gross and Buffett have corresponded with each other, and of course they know each other the way the public does, through their actions and their writings. They admire each other. Both base their investment decisions on their evaluation of a security's fundamental value. And both base their investment models on a structure that greatly increases the odds they will be successful. In Buffett's case, structure is the insurance company; it generates enormous cash flows that he is free to invest as he sees fit, without having to answer to anybody, such as quarterly earnings-fixated analysts. In Gross's case, the structure is quite different (and much less immune to quarterly carping because Gross is accountable to his investors, whereas Buffett is accountable only to himself). The PIMCO concept of structured portfolios is integral to its investment model and to its success, and is discussed at length later in this book. But in each case the men have devised an investment plan that tilts the odds in their own favor.

They invest in different markets, of course: Buffett mainly in equities and Gross entirely in fixed income. Their approaches are utterly dissimilar. Gross measures the "long term" in years, Buffett in decades. Gross trades frequently, Buffett very little. Gross takes what financial markets term a "top down" view, investment decisions made according to an overall assessment of industries and sectors rather than individual companies. Buffett is a "bottom up" investor, choosing individual securities almost without regard to their industry. He has owned a stake in Washington Post Company since before Watergate; its main rivals, The New York Times and Dow Jones, publisher of the *Wall Street Journal*, have been miserable stocks. But Gross and Buffett's shared love of real value makes them compatible. When PIMCO privately published a compendium of many of Gross's "Investment Outlooks," his monthly market musings, Buffett wrote: "Each month, I eagerly look forward to Bill Gross's commentaries. The prose is lively, the logic flawless and the insights valuable. It's going to be a delight to have his views collected in a volume to which I can readily refer."

If Gross is compatible with the world's most famous equity investor, he is less so with that field's now-retired No. 2, Peter Lynch. Gross is, in his own words, "obsessively competitive," and he simply cannot grasp someone turning his back on the field, as Lynch did when he suddenly retired in 1990. Lynch has said he retired to devote more time to his family and to philanthropy, which are two of Gross's passions. Gross will not retire, though, until he has worn out his seat on the trading floor. In 2002, Gross called Lynch's early retirement "chicken shit," and has not changed his mind.

Gross does share with Lynch, as well as Buffett, however, an informed skepticism of the Efficient Markets Theory. In its broadest sense, the theory advocates that information about public securities is so widely available and so diligently followed that the prices of large companies fairly and consistently reflect their actual value. In effect, every investor is an arbitrageur, prepared in an instant to swoop down on a stock or bond that has been mispriced by the marketplace, who then buys or sells it in sufficient quantity to quickly bring it back to fair value. (We will ignore companies such as Enron, MCI WorldCom, and ImClone for purposes of this discussion.) The logical expression of Efficient Markets is indexing; more often than not, an unguided assortment of securities chosen to represent a marketplace—big-capitalization U.S. stocks, in the case of the S&P 500—will deliver greater total returns than actively managed portfolios that specialize in the same kinds of securities. Managers make mistakes; indices do not. Managers are expensive; indexing is cheap. Thanks due to the mantra of the Efficient Markets Theory, drummed into the heads of eager listeners by the army of consultants who advise pension funds all across the country, Vanguard Group has become the nation's second-largest fund complex (after Fidelity) on the strength of its index funds. Dimensional Fund Advisors—whose most famous outside investor is Arnold Schwartzenegger—is entirely devoted to indexing, although it creates custom benchmarks in place of the common type. In the 1990s, the Vanguard 500 Index Fund outperformed 80 percent of mutual funds investing in the same kind of stocks. In my career as a financial writer, I have had the occasion to interview four Nobel laureates in economics. I have asked each of them about their personal portfolios, and in every case have been told that their core assets were invested in Vanguard index funds.

Against this orthodoxy stand the market beaters: Gross, Buffett, and Lynch. In his excellent study *The Warren Buffett Way* (John Wiley & Sons, 1997), author and money manager Robert G. Hagstrom notes that the Omaha legend's singular achievements do not shake the faith of Efficient Markets theorists. They dismiss Buffett, and thus by implication Gross, as five-sigma events—occurrences which, statistically, are so rare as to be immaterial.

Gross, as thorough a master of statistics as any MBA, says the finance professors are misled by their own ignorance. "There's a certain amount of logic to this theory, particularly in today's heavily wired, information-laden markets, but it fails to take into consideration investors' psychology," he wrote in *Bill Gross on Investing*. The market pendulum never swings obliviously from bull to bear; it is driven to speculative excess—in Internet stocks in 1999 and in Treasury bonds in 2003—by investors' greed, and then tumbles when their fear overwhelms them. As explained in Chapter Four, Gross's investing heroes were fabulously successful in large measure because they understood and countered these emotions. Gross himself has devoted a considerable amount of energy to doing the same in his own investment process. He advises you to do likewise, arguing that unless you can, you are condemned to—in that most roasted of the market's chestnuts—buy high and sell low.

———————◆———————

Even novices at the stock market know that the money to be made in the markets comes in two forms: capital appreciation (when stocks go up and you sell them) and dividends (payments most companies make out to their stockholders). The combination of the two is considered the stock's total return.[1] But for decades many investors failed to

———————

[1]Many individual equity investors focus on tax issues, and focus more on "after-tax total return" than "pre-tax total return."

consider that bonds bring in two types of revenue as well. Just as with a stock, an individual bond's total return comes from capital appreciation (or depreciation) as well as yield.

Odd as it seems today, when Gross entered the business in 1971 the typical professional bond investor (such as a bank trust officer) looked at bond returns the same way a widow or orphan would—generated by interest only. Bonds were bought when they were issued at par, or 100 cents for each dollar of face amount, and held until they matured, usually in 10 or 30 years. Affixed to the side of bond certificates were coupons, which were clipped off every six months and mailed to the issuer for that half-year's interest payment. When the bond matured, an amount of 100 cents was returned, and that was that. Bank trust departments were staffed with fraternity brothers whose handicaps were dangerously close to their IQs. As recently as the 1980s, the proverbial glass ceiling shunted women portfolio managers into fixed income where, it was thought by the gray men upstairs, they could do little harm (and nobody could do much good).

As anyone knows who watched their bond portfolio sink in June and July, 2003, when yields on the 10-year Treasury note leaped 40 percent in six weeks, from 3.11 percent to 4.41 percent, bond prices (which move inversely with yield, as explained in Chapter Five) are not fixed. They change minute by minute. Usually such changes are small, but over time bond prices move like chessmen, responding to events and informed anticipation of events that are increasingly global. In the summer of 2003, Treasuries were deflating a bubble that had formed earlier in the year, when investors had misread the recovering economy and Federal Reserve signals about monetary policy. Active total-return investors like PIMCO had been selling Treasuries (though not as much as they wished they had) and interest-sensitive mortgage pass-through bonds as the bubble formed.

There are a number of ways that a bond investor can actively manage a portfolio of fixed-income securities; they are explained later in this book. They are: diversification, managing maturities as events change, and moving within and among disparate bond sectors, such as governments, mortgages, corporates and international. The inspiration for these management decisions has to come from somewhere, however, and at PIMCO Gross has woven inspiration into the fabric of the firm's strategy. It takes two forms: *secular* and *cyclical*.

The first is a positioning of the core portfolio along lines that have the least resistance to fundamental long-term trends in the economy, society, and geopolitics. For Gross's purposes, "long term" means three to five years; forecasting anything further into the future than that diminishes confidence. (Reread George Orwell's *1984* or watch Stanley Kubrick's *2001: A Space Odyssey* again if you disagree. In the film, Kubrick's moonship was operated by Pan Am, a company name that disappeared from the Earth decades before the purported journey in the film.)

Because economists' word for "long term" is "secular," Gross and his team refer to the analysis of long-term trends as *secular analysis*. They solicit the advice of experts to help them spot trends and anticipate what may happen in the years ahead; these trends can be like waves running through the world economy, shifts in the workings of the system that change everything for a long period of time. For instance, one of the most profound demographic changes of the moment is the aging of the U.S. populations—and continental Europe's average age is rising at an even more rapid pace than it is here. Gross has used this trend to increase his holdings in companies within the medical care and pharmaceutical industries. He is not spotting equities, looking for growth stocks, or spotting future demand in the way veteran stock-pickers do. Instead, he looks for factors that lessen the credit risks of bond issuers whose paper he holds. To his eagle eyes, the "graying of America" might suggest that a bond issue of a giant hospital chain might be a safer place to store cash than, say, paper issued by a national toy manufacturer.

Balancing the analysis of secular trends is what Gross terms "cyclical" trends. These are the changes that affect the market over much shorter periods; PIMCO looks at them formally every quarter, and informally every day. Examples include the changes in the federal funds rate (set by the Federal Reserve); the impact of new producer price index figures, nervousness or relief in the markets caused by the situation in the Middle East—in other words, the minute-by-minute tremors and waves that affect the credit and stock markets every day. Gross's successful foray into Treasury bonds in 2000, when he guessed that stocks were wildly overpriced and the economy was about to crash, was a short term, or cyclical, play designed to benefit from events that would play themselves out in a year or so. His reaction to 2003's rate rise was similarly pegged to events, rather than to the firm's secular view. Even as they dumped massive amounts of mortgage bonds for short-term cyclical reasons, Gross and PIMCO remained wedded to mortgage bonds over the long term for secular reasons.

Again, their reasoning is based on the aging baby boomers: if fewer home mortgages are taken out in coming years, as fewer people replace the more numerous baby boomers, mortgage bond prices could rise. This may seem counterintuitive to readers, especially those who are equity investors. The stock prices of companies like Fannie Mae and Freddie Mac, each of which is a publicly owned corporation whose shares trade on the New York Stock Exchange, would be hit hard if mortgage demand went down. These companies were created by Congress to stand behind the home mortgage market, increasing the volume of available debt and thus lowering its price, by packaging home loans into securities that find buyers like PIMCO. If their volume decreased, so would their revenue and their earnings; if the Street heard that mortgage demand was crashing, the shrinking business and lower fees would force the market to push down its stock prices.

Bond holders can take a different view because they have no equity stake in the issuer. While stocks have unlimited upside (they can double, quadruple, and even—as with Peter Lynch—soar 2,500 percent), the only upside to a bond, in the words of PIMCO Fed watcher Paul McCulley, "is that you get your money back." This ability to get your money back is not affected by the question of whether the business is shrinking or rising, unless the company looks like it might go out of business and the bondholders therefore face default risk. We can assume Fannie and Freddie would not pose credit risk to investors. A lower demand for mortgages will not stop these companies from retaining their gilt-edged credit ratings, because their assets are implicitly backed by the U.S. government.

However, the lower demand for mortgages would mean that Fannie and Freddie were issuing fewer bonds. Their mortgage securities would automatically become scarcer than before. As bond prices react to supply and demand just like everything else, a scarcity of new issues could push up the prices of old mortgage issues.

Currently, mortgage bonds yield about 2 percentage points more than Treasuries of comparable maturity, yet from most perspectives they are virtually as safe. This premium, which bond investors call "carry," is as close to free money as financial markets offer.[2] It reflects the fact that, in our current economy, we are still in a huge real estate boom and mortgage pass-through bonds are so abundant: they constitute a $6 trillion marketplace. If such bonds were scarce, the prices of the previously issued bonds would rise and the yields of the newly issued bonds would fall: Fannie Mae and Freddie Mac would have a far easier time selling their newly issued bonds, and they would not therefore have to bother to pay out such a large carry to buyers. However, the price of their older bonds, paying out coupons at a higher rate, would rise. Instead of owning billions in bonds worth 100 cents today, PIMCO could own billions worth 102 cents next year, 104 the year after that, and so on.

---

[2]Built into a mortgage bond's carry is a premium investors demand for its negative convexity; that is, its perverse reaction to changes in interest rates, owing to how they impact its prepayment risk. In benign markets this risk is low, but it rises dramatically when rates are going up, because prepayments decline and duration increases, eating into carry.

There are two lessons to take from this. First, the perspectives of the stock investor and the bond investor can be almost diametrically opposite. The former relishes a roaring economy, because it means stronger earnings. The latter is frazzled; eventually the Federal Reserve will "take away the punchbowl" in the form of raising interest rates, which depress bond prices. Yet, bondholders do not usually mind dips or downturns in the economy as they can make their currently held bonds more valuable. They are nervous about credit risk but less so than stockholders: common stock is usually worthless in a bankruptcy. Bonds survive, though, and sometimes even are transmuted into more valuable equity in the reorganized firm. In comic book terms, stock investors are like Li'l Abner, perpetually basking in sunlight and optimism. Bond investors are like Joe Btfsplk, the fellow who walks around under a rain cloud. The former hope for riches; the latter worry about getting their money back.

⸺•⸺

So what are the basic elements of Bill Gross's strategy, the building blocks of what he and PIMCO call Total Return investing? The best way, I found, to answer this question, was to ask the Bond King what he considers the most important lessons he has learned in his career.

It will seem extraordinary to readers who work in the investment industry that Bill Gross regards his experience at the blackjack table as his basic training for professional investing. The belief that placing money in the financial markets is not "gambling" is so ingrained that it might as well be the fundamental proposition on which the whole investing industry rests and uses to justify itself. Industrial giant J. Pierpont Morgan once walked away from a lucrative deal because the man who offered it casually described it as a gamble, and the great man froze in insult at the word. While Gross's belief that gambling and investing share certain traits is therefore dire heresy, one cannot deny that his genius began to emerge when he saw the parallels between the credit markets and that green table at the Four Queens. To say that he relates investing to gambling is not to say that he is anything like the average gambler: foolish, wildly undisciplined, chancy. The parallels come from the *method* of the professional gambler, the probability theory employed by the gambler, (and by the world's top mathematicians)—not from the louche spirit, the stale smoke, or the desperation of the poor soul who has spent too much time at Foxwoods.

At blackjack, Gross discovered a way to assess and evaluate the probability of future events (what investors usually term "risk"): He divided the play of the cards into two paradigms that echo what he now calls secular and cyclical analysis. The subject of his cyclical analysis at the Four Queens was seemingly basic: What card would the dealer turn up next?

In a sense, blackjack is all about the answer to this question. If you hold a 15, you would draw if you think the next card is likely to be a 6 or lower. However, you would stay if you have a reason for thinking the next card is likely to be a 7 or higher (you would also factor in an analysis of the dealer's turned-up card and the chance that the dealer will subsequently draw a good or bad card). The cards as they are dealt are cyclical challenges; they can belie the odds. Similarly, investors have no way of knowing in advance what the next durable goods orders reported by the Department of Commerce will be, when we might face a terrorist attack, or when something destabilizing and nerve-wracking might happen in the Korean peninsula. The best investors and casino players, however, try to develop the ability to predict some of the cyclical challenges that life may throw at them. If you try, as Gross does, to develop the skill to know if the next card is likely to be low or high, you will enjoy success. You may be frequently wrong but if you average out on top, you are winning.

At the Four Queens table, the cards remaining in the shoe created the long-term, as opposed to short-term, odds; they represent the secular challenges. Long before these cards are dealt, the adroit player can anticipate what they will be, or at least whether they are more likely to be low, encouraging the player to draw, or high, to stand pat. While on occasion sudden cyclical changes will happen to make the markets react very quickly—often creating the temporary sense that everything has changed—the long-term future can be best predicted by looking at the secular changes going on in the country and the world.

Investors can vastly improve their investing acumen by learning to predict, with some accuracy, the secular changes coming down the pike. This skill is key to Gross's stunning record of success. And, it is easier to develop—for those of us who are not Miss Cleo—than the art of predicting the fickle curve balls that tend to emerge from the quotidian, cyclical universe that keeps the news industry alive and often surprises us all.

Bill Gross discovered three basic lessons from his months at the tables. First, gamblers learn to spread their risk. The cards run hot and cold; even the best blackjack players will endure periods when the cards are running against them, and they have to hold onto enough chips to survive these droughts. In investing terms, those chips are capital—when you run out of it you are done. Even more important is the second lesson: Know the risks that exist, quantify them, and try to predict their effect on the card table. Gross applied this lessons when he used his card counting system to assess the probability of future deals of face cards, aces, and deuces. Third, and a seeming violation of the risk rule, is this: When the odds favor the player, the best bet is a big bet.

Gross thinks his first big lesson, spreading risk, came from his decision to stay in the game, to never bet so much that his capital would dissipate too quickly. In his Vegas days, Gross found that the inevitable boring periods when no discernable patterns developed were interrupted by flurries of action during which big sums could be won or lost. At the tables of the Fremont and Four Queens casinos, he began a regimen of probing a new dealer or a new deck with small, consistent bets and waiting patiently for the odds to reveal themselves. When they were against him, he wagered two dollars and accepted his losses as a cost of doing business. But when they were with him, he made bigger bets, and bigger still the more the odds favored him over the dealer. Even when he lost big, however, he stayed in the game, reverting to his two-dollar bets.

As a money manager, Gross today sees himself in the same way that PIMCO describes itself: as an "investor for all seasons," plugging along whether markets are up or down, not retreating to the sidelines. This is called going to cash, in market parlance. Going to cash, or timing the market, is a skill that only a handful of investors possess. One of Gross's few rivals as a fixed-income investor is Robert Rodriguez of First Pacific Advisors in Los Angeles. He manages the only intermediate-term, high-quality bond fund (FPA New Income) that has not had a single losing year in the last 20. Rodriguez will hold a third of his port-folio or more in cash when he feels he does not have more attractive choices. Gross, however, recognizes he lacks this sense.

Making big bets in the right circumstances is a crucial aspect of gambling but it carries within it the seeds of destruction. A streak of bad cards can run through a gambler's entire stake in no time at all. A professional gambler has to protect his grubstake. Gross started with only $200; a single bet amounted to 1 percent of his total assets. His parents expected him to come home: after all, inexperienced gamblers are inclined to win a few dollars and feel so flush that they quickly frit-ter everything away when the cards turn against them. As Gross's kitty grew so did his reserves; he always hewed to the rule of "gamblers ruin"—always hold 50 times your maximum bet. At PIMCO, risk management is one of the highest priorities; the firm has a phalanx of computer jockeys who do nothing else. Gross also manages risk by diversifying his portfolios very thoroughly among the various types of fixed-income securities, from Treasury notes to corporate bonds to junk and convertibles and an alphabet of derivatives. He further diver-sifies by spreading assets across a broad range of issuers to reduce the risk of any one of them.

Yet despite his discipline, Gross believes in making big bets when he thinks the odds are with him. "Do you really like a particular stock?" he wrote in his book. "Put 10 percent or so of your portfolio on it. Make that idea count. Are you confident that emerging market debt is attractive? . . . Same thing. Good ideas should not be diversified away into meaningless oblivion. If you've got fifty stocks in your portfolio, you've got too many. If you've got 10 mutual funds, you're too diversified." He practices what he preaches: Gross plunks down serious money, sometimes to the tune of a fifth of his investors' assets, with the regularity of a metronome. In 1996, he funneled 20 percent of assets into foreign bonds, which outperformed domestic paper, and also gained from overweighting mortgages. In 1998, when Russia defaulted on its sovereign debt and sent global securities markets reeling, Gross's portfolios flourished because he had shifted to Treasuries, which surged in a "flight to quality." In 2000, he slashed corporate bond holdings just as the great bear market in equities—and corporate earnings—was about to begin, and stampeded into the Treasury market ahead of the government itself, which began buying back bonds to accommodate a burgeoning surplus. In the middle of 2001, after the Federal Reserve had cut interest rates six times and the market decided further cuts were unlikely, Gross bet the opposite way, scoring big when another five rate cuts for a total of 2 percentage points rained down in succeeding months, prompting a Morningstar analyst to write, "His ability to add value with interest-rate bets over time has been nothing short of astonishing."

The bets do not always succeed: Also in 1996, for example, Gross wasted a good share of profits from foreign and mortgage bonds on a Treasury bet that rates would fall, and they did not. In 1999, the fund slipped into red ink to the tune of 0.28 percent (when the rest of the market was flat to slightly higher), again because Gross had extended average maturities of his portfolios and instead of cutting rates, as it had the prior year, the Fed began raising them.

Most of Gross's rivals in bond investing are loathe to make big bets, precisely because they can backfire. But most of his rivals also lack the gambler's edge that Gross acquired in his early twenties. In gambling and investing, he says: "The instincts are the same. My gambling—which I didn't think was gambling; I thought it was investing—my gambling required extensive money management qualities. I had to know how much I could risk, because if I risked too much a streak of bad luck could wipe me out in 24 hours and send me home to Mommy and Daddy." Today PIMCO's risks are not so hedged that they cannot make an impact on a portfolio's bottom line, but they are well hedged.

Gross is legendarily unafraid to take huge positions in securities favored by the odds. In the fall of 2001, PIMCO bought $45 billion worth of mortgage bonds. Scott Simon, PIMCO's point man on mortgages, says "they were pretty much as cheap as they had ever been." Refinancings were beginning to surge, which alarmed the market: prepayments on home loans are like a call on corporate bonds, shortening their effective life at the worst possible time, because they ride the back of falling interest rates. This means that investors get their money back when they want it least. Bonds were cheap because other investors were dumping them, driving their yields to 200 basis points, or hundredths of a percentage point, over comparable Treasuriess. In the ensuing four months, when it became clear the refinancing boom was not devastating the market as much as it had feared, mortgage bond prices soared so much that "it would have been their best year ever," Simon says. The market "didn't want them at 200 but they bought at 140." They bought from PIMCO; it closed out the bet, selling $45 billion and booking a profit of 2 percent on the transaction, over and above the yields of the bonds while PIMCO owned them. "Mortgages behave like the Nasdaq," Simon explains. "When they're expensive, everybody wants them, and when they're cheap, everybody wants to sell."

Gross was gambling with nearly a fifth of PIMCO's total assets under management at the time, which makes him a rare bond investor. The typical bond fund of the PIMCO Total Return type owns 295 names, according to Morningstar, meaning average positions are traces of one percentage point, not twenty of them. But the yields on the bonds signaled to Gross that the odds were heavily on his side, and he was right.

Despite his willingness to make big bets, Gross's focus on capital preservation—PIMCO Total Return has actually lost money in only two full years of its existence, one a negligible 0.28 percent loss, the other a significant fall of 3.58 percent—leads him to control risk in his portfolios obsessively. This is far harder than it sounds. Bonds are no so much discrete securities as they are baskets of options. Each of them carries its own risks as well as rewards. With mortgage bonds, for example, prepayment risk is huge. In the summer of 2003, when long interest rates backed up so suddenly and dramatically, the average duration of mortgages in the Lehman Brothers Aggregate Bond Index tripled to three years. Duration is akin to maturity, except it is a mathematically precise measurement of the degree of maturity risk; long bonds are riskier than short ones because there is more time for things to go wrong.

One of PIMCO's most adroit early moves as a firm was to attract Chris Dialynas, an options-pricing expert, nearly two decades before his mentor, Myron Scholes, won the Nobel Prize in Economic Sciences for his work. When Dialynas graduated from the University of Chicago's Graduate School of Business in 1980, he had 30 job offers, and only one offered lower pay than PIMCO. He was impressed at the scope of the work PIMCO offered, however, and indeed has become one of Gross's most trusted partners. One of the first assignments he was given was to analyze the pitch of an aggressive young salesman of below-investment-grade debt named Michael Milken, of a firm called Drexel Burnham Lambert. During the 1980s Milken would revolutionize the marketplace for bonds that quickly became known as junk, ultimately going to prison and sending his firm into receivership. When he called on PIMCO, however, he was on his meteoric way up. Dialynas did not like the numbers that Milken's crunching produced, though, and recommended that PIMCO pass. It did.

Risk control is part of a process, a regimen, designed to help Gross control emotion, which he calls investing's "dangerous drug." Emotions run high on Wall Street; its billions engender greed on a scale that would shame King Midas, and a fear of losing them that is even greater. Nobody is immune. One of Gross's heroes, Jesse Livermore, went bust eight times, despite his best efforts to control his passions. Gross himself is no less vulnerable. He remembers being frozen like a deer in the headlights in October 1987, when bonds as well as stocks crashed; had he not been seized by the same dread as everyone else, PIMCO might have made millions in the ensuing bond rally.

Gross recognizes this limitation, however, and his investment process includes a variety of tools intended to take emotion out of decision making to the greatest extent practicable. It can never be removed entirely. PIMCO's Mark Kiesel remembers a different October, that of 2002, when stocks and everything connected to them, including the bonds of their issuers, had plunged to lows that likely marked the absolute bottom of the bear market. (Only time will tell if future declines are worse.) "All these bonds in all these companies were trading at historically wide spreads" to risk-free Treasuries, Kiesel recalls. Fully half his portfolio was tanking. "You've got a rifle pointed at your head, every day," he says.

Kiesel, however, was protected from panic selling by PIMCO's investment process, which is founded in secular analysis. October's lows came when investors who had been hoping for economic recovery threw in the towel. Officially, the recession that had begun in March 2001 was still under way; unemployment was rising. Although PIMCO believed in its secular judgment that the era of expansive economic growth expired with the end of the twentieth century, the company had adopted the contradictory cyclical view that growth would be slow, not absent.

Indeed, gross domestic product growth was positive, although feeble. When Kiesel was grilled by Gross and the other members of PIMCO's Investment Committee, he had to defend his individual choices, not the premise that high-quality corporate bonds were desirable investments—a sure sign that management and Gross agreed with his analysis that things were only temporarily in flux. In the end, PIMCO's portfolios rode out the storm, which turned out to be more like a wave or ripple. Kiesel's performance benefited from the subsequent rally. The following summer, when the National Bureau of Economic Research finally decided the recession was over, it dated recovery to November, 2001—just eight months after the recession had begun. The secular process provided the foundation for Kiesel's judgment and PIMCO's, that appearances were deceptive that October.

I devote a considerable portion of this book to Gross's secular orientation because it is so important. It is arrived at and maintained with considerable intellectual rigor, but it is not difficult to grasp. Demographic trends—a key element—are documented by a host of public agencies, notably the Bureau of the Census and the population division of the Department of Economic and Social Affairs of the United Nations Secretariat. These trends give birth to many of the most controversial social debates of our time. Aging baby boomers are demanding free prescription drugs in retirement, but the number of Americans aged 65 and older is expected to increase 58 percent in the next quarter century to nearly one in five of the entire population—from less than one in eight now. Europe's powerful labor unions are striking to combat tighter reins on older people's pension benefits, but the demographic tide is even stronger there than here. In Germany, 16 percent of the population is aged—compared to 12 percent in the United States—and that is projected to soar to 26 percent by 2030. In Japan, the prospects are even more dolorous: a surge to 30 percent of the population, a near doubling of today's 17 percent.

The elderly have far less disposable income than the young—around 40 percent less, according to most estimates. In a nation where consumerism accounts for two-thirds of GDP, 40 cents less on every dollar spent by that fifth of the population in retirement will subtract correspondingly from economic growth. The implications spread like ripples on a pond. Social Security responsibilities will rise, dragging up taxes. The tax burden will fall on fewer people. The available pool of investible capital will simultaneously shrink; retirees are "dis-savers," drawing from their savings to live. All this is true of the developed world, but in the less-developed world contrary trends are taking place, with populations growing and becoming younger. When Bill Gross recommends investing in emerging markets, he is recognizing the power of these inexorable forces: a secular trend.

Similarly, the forces of inflation and its evil twin, deflation, are at war around the globe. The bursting of the Treasury bubble in 2003 came in part because the Fed decided to abandon its generation-long fight against inflation in order to joust with its opposite; a pro-inflation central bank is an oxymoron, but this is the operative stance of the U.S. government today. And it is not unreasonable. China and India are exporting deflation to the developed world with every container ship. They are even exporting it over the phone: India is selling itself as the world's call center, where 800 numbers are answered by people who earn a fraction of the U.S. wage but are trained to speak idiomatic American English and even to know local sports scores in the regions they serve. Deflation has been an important secular theme at PIMCO, but that is evolving; the Fed's pro-inflation stance is calling into question the firm's emphasis on deflation.

His keen focus on secular trends and his ability to anticipate cyclical moves are what has made Gross the Bond King. In the later sections of this book, I show you how to imitate the Bond King's keen eye. But let us first look deeper into the people who influenced Gross's beliefs, the men who became his mentors in the financial markets. The writings of three great gurus changed Gross's views and informed his deep knowledge of the markets; I call them the Three Magi in honor of the role their gifts played in Gross's rise to success.

CHAPTER 3

The Gifts of the Magi

When you enter Bill Gross's office at The Beach, the first thing you notice are three framed portraits behind his desk. Every day, he brings to the office his keen insight into and analysis of the world economy, along with the recommendations and ideas of the experts at PIMCO's secular conferences. He applies this knowledge with lightning speed to the blinking numbers on the Bloombergs. Beyond the immediacy of Gross's ideas about U.S. gross domestic product or the economy of Southeast Asia, however, lies a deep and serious philosophy, epitomized by those black-and-white photographs on his office wall. These are the images of Gross's investment heroes, the men who bolstered his will and determination, the men he partially credits for his success. The three portraits overlook his wiry frame and tapping fingers with silent approval. They are like the biblical Magi: each one made a contribution to Gross's investment ideology and each one has something to offer individual bond investors.

Gross's heroes have a number of characteristics in common. All three men were born in the nineteenth century. One of them, J.Pierpont Morgan, survives in public memory, but the other two are lesser known: Bernard Baruch and Jesse Livermore. Baruch, though he established a huge fortune in the stock market, spent most of his life in public service and is mainly remembered for something he did not even say: "Buy when there is blood in the streets." (It was a Rothschild who said these words about the streets of Paris.) Livermore is a character straight out of Damon Runyon, a wise-cracking stock speculator of the 1920s who would not have been out of place in "Guys and Dolls," and might indeed have romanced the lead actress.

Each of these men was a master of the business world, possessed of clear vision and indomitable self-confidence. Each sought to eliminate emotion from their considerations, to steel themselves against the temporary passions that rule markets in the short term. Each saw investing in strategic terms and while they were quick to take advantage of the opportunities that came their way, their greatest successes came after long study and careful preparation.

One can see elements of Gross in all three: Morgan was an empire builder; Baruch was an athlete; Livermore had a wry and penetrating sense of humor. The three were—like Gross—prodigies at mathematics, able to calculate advantages faster than their business rivals. All held themselves accountable to a high ethical standard. Baruch was several inches taller than Gross but exactly the same weight; like the latter, the former moved to a big city from a distant rural area at the age of 10—a move that left an indelible impression on him. Both men married women of different religious faiths. Livermore insisted on funereal quiet while at work, Baruch and Livermore were flamboyant gamblers, and Morgan saw his highest calling as establishing a firm that would survive him: the three Magi are clearly not just paragons to Gross—they share deep commonalities with him.

Bill Gross remembers picking up a book called *Reminiscences of a Stock Operator* shortly after joining PIMCO in the early 1970s. This barely fictionalized biography of Livermore was nominally written by Edwin Lefèvre, another stock operator and author of the 1920s. Gross was absorbed first by the candor of the subject, who in the book is called Larry Livingston. The character is brutally honest about his own failures as an investor, but unstinting in sharing his insights into, most of all, human nature. Gross had been a psychology major in college, and he recognized in Livermore a master of human psychology. "Livermore speaks to knowing yourself," Gross says now. "Before you can understand a marketplace you have to begin with an understanding of yourself and your own particular foibles and eccentricities." The Livermore quote Gross has on his wall is this: "In actual practice, an investor has to guard against many things, and most of all against himself."

Along with Bernard Baruch and Joseph P. Kennedy, father of the future president John F. Kennedy, Livermore was blamed for the Great Crash of 1929. Unlike those men, he never recovered from that calumny. But his formative years, the ones described in Lefèvre's book, have been an inspiration to many of today's Wall Street leaders, including investment managers Martin Zweig and Kenneth L. Fisher. Richard Smitten wrote in *Jesse Livermore: World's Greatest Stock Trader* (John Wiley & Sons, 2001), "There is no question that *Reminiscences* is one of the best financial books ever written."

Jesse Lauriston Livermore was born in a rural hamlet in Massachusetts on July 26, 1877. His father, Hiram, was a dour and unhappy man and a poor farmer, losing his land as well as his son's affection. His mother, Laura, was much more optimistic; Jesse took after her personality. In grammar school, he revealed himself as a mathematics prodigy, proudly proclaiming ever after that he had mastered three years' of math studies in one. The ease and accuracy with which he could remember numbers and manipulate them in his head was the underpinning of his financial success and considerable fame.

When Jesse was 13, however, his father pulled him out of school, telling him education was wasted on a farmer. Yet the truth was that farming was wasted on Jesse. In only a few months, staked to the tune of five dollars by his mother, he fled to Boston, where he found work as a chalkboard boy in a Paine Webber brokerage office. The office manager, Livermore would later say, had been impressed by his self-confidence, which was indeed one of his most important traits.

In that era, securities prices were entered manually on green chalkboards in brokers' offices. Besides being meticulous, Livermore was quick to grasp patterns in changing prices of individual securities. He did not know at the time what produced them, and indeed he remained a tape reader rather than a fundamental analyst throughout his career. But he was quick to detect patterns in the numbers. When his work was done for the day, he wrote down all the stock quotations remaining on the board, each day comparing them with his records and analyzing the patterns they revealed. What they showed him was that stock price changes had *momentum*. When they were rising, they tended to continue to rise, and vice versa. Ultimately he was to learn that this momentum could be turned to an investor's advantage. He called it "following the path of least resistance."

Livermore lived frugally and saved like a miser to build enough capital to invest. He could not afford a conventional brokerage account. He did not have the net worth that legitimate firms required, nor the capital to buy and sell "round" 100-share lots of stocks, themselves often priced around par ($100). At the time, however, Boston teemed with "bucket shops." These were a kind of gamblers' den disguised as legitimate brokerages and run by organized mobs. They allowed investors—"suckers" in their own eyes and, quickly, in Livermore's—to buy small lots of stock, and even single shares, with just 10 percent equity and 90 percent margin. In these private, over-the-counter exchanges, real securities prices were posted on their chalkboards in close to real time, but instead of actually trading shares on the exchange the shops kept a private book. Buyers were wiped out when prices of their shares fell 10 percent, and the bucket shops conspired to fleece their customers by frequently delaying posting of fresh quotes so as to lull them into making foolish bets. For example, in the case of a stock whose price had steadily surged from $90 to $100, the bucket shops would raise the quote slowly, and pause it at $95. This would lead some investors to short the issue, expecting a retreat. In the actual advance, they were skinned of nearly all their money. "Since suckers always lose money when they gamble in stocks," Livermore remarks in *Reminiscences*, "you'd think these fellows would run what you might call a legitimate illegitimate business. But they don't."

Livermore himself developed something of a sixth sense about trading. It displayed itself throughout his life, and not always to his advantage. He managed to lose so much money buying swampland in Florida and taking flyers that he lost millions of dollars. But in the bucket shops he was nearly infallible. Within months of taking the Paine Webber job he quit to become a full-time speculator. He amassed a total of $1,000, and earned the sobriquet "boy plunger" on his way to being barred from every bucket shop in Boston.

At the age of 20, he went to Manhattan and opened a genuine brokerage account with E.F. Hutton. He traded patiently, using the skills he had developed in the bucket shops—and they quickly backfired. In the bucket shop, he bought and sold at the price on the board, which was (usually) fresh from the ticker. He never lost more than 10 percent of his capital on a single bet. In the brokerage office, however, real trades were often executed at very different prices than those on the board: clerks had to enter them manually and run down the street to the exchange and hand them off to a trading desk. This took so much time that Livermore often paid 10 percent more for shares than he had planned, and sold them for less when they were falling. Also, Hutton gave 50 percent margin, so his losses were vastly greater than he had planned on. Within months he was busted. Hutton himself offered to stake the young speculator—his trading commissions were considerable—but Livermore asked instead for a loan of $1,000 to go back to the bucket shops. Hutton gave him the loan and Livermore took the train to St. Louis, where in three days he parlayed it into $3,800, was barred again, and returned to New York. He paid Hutton back but declined his offer to re-open his account. Livermore had figured out he needed a different system for legitimate trading. Bucket shops could be taken for quick, small moves in a stock. Wall Street was too cumbersome for that. So he crossed the Hudson River to a freshly opened bucket shop in Hoboken, New Jersey. (New York City itself, although it turned a blind eye to all manner of vice, never allowed bucket shops—possibly because its powerful brokerage industry did not want the competition.) Although he was so successful that he was quickly barred, he recruited a friend to front for him and racked up a personal stake of $10,000 by the time he was 23. By the standards of his family he was rich, and began to spend less parsimoniously. He also married a young pretty girl named Nettie Jordan. They soon separated when he went broke the second of what was to be eight times.

It was Livermore's fate to develop one of the most successful stock-trading strategies of all time (based on common sense rules) and then to violate the rules again and again. The system was simple. He was a loner; every partnership into which he entered was a disaster. He acted alone because he spurned the opinions of others. He developed the view that suckers can be divided into three classes, depending on the degree of proximity they had to true inside knowledge, but were all suckers nonetheless, because they acted on tips instead of thinking for themselves. He followed the market's momentum, going long or selling short, but greatly lengthened his time horizon, from minutes to months, in order to accommodate slow-moving, real-world trading. That in turn forced him to discern longer-term trends than the momentary movements of the bucket shops. They were still technical in nature—he did not fail to take advantage of a single significant market top or bottom between 1907 and 1929, based purely on both "the feel of the tape" and a reasoned analysis of macroeconomic conditions—but they became, to use a word Bill Gross uses in his own investment approach, "secular." As the pithy Livermore himself put it, "Men who can both be right and sit tight are uncommon."

Having gone broke twice before he become a major Wall Street player, Livermore also learned the gambler's secret—always keep enough powder dry to play again. Eventually he even created trusts in his boom years to protect some capital for the next bust, but even these were foiled; though he could think straight in the market, he was astonishingly disorganized in his personal life, ultimately losing everything in a tangle of divorces and mistresses. Perversely, the Livermore quote that Gross has on his office wall was the dictum he violated so often that his life ended in ruin. "The only time I really ever lost money was when I broke my own rules," Smitten reports that Livermore told one of his sons, but he lost all his money anyway.

Livermore's trading strategy was a combination of art and science. Once he had decided to make a play, whether long or short, he first committed 20 percent of what he planned to be the eventual investment. If the stock behaved as he expected—rising when he was long, falling when he was short—he invested a second 20 percent, and then a third. At this point, it was common for the target stock to stabilize, as long investors took profits and shorts bailed out. If the stock broke against him after this stabilization phase, he would sell out the position, trying never to take losses greater than 10 percent of his total planned investment. If it broke in his favor, he made the final 40 percent bet and waited patiently, often for months, to realize his profits. The real money, he often said, was made "in the waiting." He rode out positions until he reached what he called Pivotal Points, which he explained in his own book, published in 1940, *How to Trade in Stocks*. Pivotal Points are moments when the direction of a security's price changes. Only the market can announce when these points are reached—the usual signal is extraordinarily heavy trading volume. Taken together, Livermore's system was intended to take ego and emotion out of the calculation, since Livermore well knew he was just as vulnerable to emotion as any other investor. In fact, he was more vulnerable, owing to chronic bouts of depression that eventually would lead him to take his own life.

By 1906, Livermore had mastered legitimate investing and his trading account was worth more than a quarter million dollars. He decided to take a vacation to Atlantic City, New Jersey, and as was his custom he closed out all his positions before leaving town. While walking down the Boardwalk on a blustery April afternoon, he and a friend strolled into the branch office of the E.F. Hutton firm. Livermore took the tape between his fingers and began to study it. He could never explain how intimately the tape spoke to him. He intellectually understood its two most important lessons—how rising prices and higher volume can indicate that a stock is under accumulation, and how high volume and falling prices can signal it is being disposed of—but the hunches it gave him were a mystery to him his whole life. As he began examining trades in the hottest stock of the moment, Union Pacific, the tape fairly screamed to him something totally illogical: UP was a short. He immediately shorted 1,000 shares, with both the clerk and his friend trying to talk him out of it. He confessed he did not know why he was so convinced—he later called the episode his "spooky story"—but after the two other men had ticked off all the pluses of a wonderful stock in a wonderful market, he shorted another 2,000 shares, and then yet another 2,000, for a total of 5,000. He then declared an end to his vacation and returned to New York on April 17—one day before the San Francisco earthquake.

Union Pacific had thousands of miles of track in the Western United States, but when word of the tragedy reached Manhattan, Union Pacific and the market in general actually went up. Word had spread of Livermore's short position, and his rivals delighted that the speculator's position was becoming expensive. Livermore was undeterred, however. He shorted another 5,000 shares of UP. As the magnitude of the disaster and its impact on the economy of the West unfolded, however, UP shares cratered. Livermore's hunch netted him a profit of $250,000. Ed Hutton personally congratulated the speculator on his coup. And then, that summer, Livermore began buying UP. The tape's message to Livermore was unmistakable; somebody was accumulating UP shares very steadily. Hutton called his favorite client and told him he had inside knowledge that Livermore was being played for a chump. In fact, Hutton asserted, UP shares were being manipulated so insiders could sell without taking a bath. The story was not far-fetched; Livermore himself engaged in stock manipulation on a large scale more than once; it was not illegal. In this instance Livermore was convinced he was right, but Hutton wounded his vanity. Livermore sold his entire UP stake with only minor profits, just before the railroad announced a huge dividend. He had been right; insiders were accumulating the stock ahead of the announcement, and Livermore's buying was pushing up the price; they had duped Hutton into taking the speculator off their case. If Livermore had held, he would have reaped a profit of $50,000. He did not blame Hutton; he blamed himself for violating his own rule of avoiding "tips."

Despite this miscue, Livermore had roughly $1 million in his trading accounts, so in 1907 he sold all his positions and took a long vacation. He was well known and respected on Wall Street, but he was not yet a public figure. He went to Florida first to fish in the Gulf Stream (fishing was one of his favorite pursuits), and then to Paris. Even in France, however, he was unable to tear himself away from the market. At the peak of his career Livermore had tickers installed in his mansion, his Manhattan apartment, a vacation cottage on Lake Placid in upstate New York, a suite of rooms he took regularly at the Breaker's Hotel in Palm Beach, and aboard his yachts. While in Paris in the summer of 1907, however, he was intrigued by a copy of the European edition of the *Herald Tribune*. It reported a round of higher interest rates rippling through Europe's banks. Rates were also rising in the United States, and domestic employment was beginning to fall. Livermore quickly surmised that the stock market was ignoring a looming recession. He booked passage home and immediately began shorting stocks to the full capacity of his margin account.

A far greater figure than Livermore in the Panic of 1907 was J. Pierpont Morgan, so it is described below in the context of Morgan's illustrious career. Livermore's role in it, however, turned out to be important both to the market and to him. The Panic spread from a run on the banks to a run on Wall Street, which was heavily leveraged by margin. It climaxed on October 24, when stocks came under relentless selling pressure. At noon every trading day the city's bankers appeared at what was called the Money Post on the floor of the New York Stock Exchange, but that day it was deserted; not a single bank was willing to lend to brokers, even at interest above 150 percent. Brokers immediately began selling out margined accounts, which was virtually all of them, and the price rout accelerated. Morgan saved the day by arranging for the banks to dip into their reserves to finance the immediate crisis—and by appealing to the market's most successful short, Livermore, not to take advantage of the situation.

Livermore was never happier than when the market gushed rewards for his prescience, so on October 24 he was sitting at his desk calculating the take. He made a profit of $1 million that day, by far the biggest one-day gain of his career, but that was nothing compared to what he foresaw. Morgan had averted the immediate liquidity crisis, but in those pre-Federal Reserve days, longer-term liquidity was very much in doubt. Livermore could easily see his short portfolio blossom—profits of $10 million were almost guaranteed. $20 million was possible—maybe even $40 million. Amid these reveries he received a guest, an investment banker from a prominent firm. The man entreated him to close out his short positions and go long. He appealed to Livermore's patriotism, and made clear that he was speaking on behalf of Morgan personally. In *Reminiscences*, Livermore says, "Go back and tell Mr. Blank that I agree with him and that I fully realized the gravity of the situation even before he sent for you." And Livermore was as good as his word. In fact, the market did rally when the short selling stopped, and within days he booked profits on his long positions of an additional $2 million. Morgan's attention, he said, made him feel like "king for a moment." And when his role in helping unwind the Panic was reported in the newspapers, Livermore became a national celebrity. He was about to go broke again, but at least he was learning the lesson he in turn taught Gross: to know yourself.

In the wake of the Panic, Livermore was a major big shot. He had a 200-foot yacht and a place at the roulette table at Bradley's Beach Club in Palm Beach, the most fashionable casino of that era. Another regular there was Percy Thomas, the "Cotton King," but he could not gamble; he had gone broke in a failed speculation. He was always welcome for dinner, however, and he introduced himself to Livermore, who played commodities markets regularly. The two men hit it off, and Livermore offered to stake Thomas, but he did not want a loan—he wanted a partnership. From balmy day to balmy night, he taught Livermore everything there was to know about the cotton market. It was a lesson that proved very expensive. Aside from macroeconomic conditions, Livermore was a technical trader, and he was convinced the cotton market was washed out. He himself had been successfully speculating in wheat. But Thomas's magnetic personality, his powerful logic, and his vast command of market fundamentals seduced Livermore into abandoning the self-guided, lone wolf approach that had made him so successful. Starting small, Thomas and Livermore soon committed the speculator's entire fortune to what became a failed attack against a falling market. Livermore even sold his winning commodity—wheat—to finance the loser, violating his most fundamental rule of accepting losses but letting profits run. In the space of a few weeks Livermore was not just broke—he was $1 million in the hole. He sold his yacht and fell into a deep depression, to which he was vulnerable throughout his life, and moved to Chicago, hoping to resurrect himself in the bucket shops. Characteristically, he did not blame Thomas for his downfall. He blamed himself.

From 1908 to 1915, Livermore lived in poverty and obscurity; at one point he even filed for bankruptcy, which he considered an act of great shame because he always paid his debts. In those years he reasoned out what had made him successful, and what had cost him his fortunes. He ended his exile with a borrowed line at a brokerage firm.

War in Europe was producing huge profits for American manufacturers, and Livermore went long the market so successfully that he was soon prosperous once more. Then, as it seemed more and more likely the United States would enter the war, he went short—as did his friend, Bernard Baruch. At one point both men were grilled before Congress; short selling was seen then, as it often is now, as unpatriotic. But Livermore did so well in the First World War that he was able to pay off his creditors in the bankruptcy—even though legally he did not have to—and resume a grand lifestyle.

This included a new wife. His friend Flo Ziegfeld, the Broadway impresario, introduced him to a petite actress named Dorothy Wendt, who was appearing in the Ziegfeld Follies. The two hit it off. Livermore had long been separated from his previous wife and divorced her in 1917. The following year he married Wendt. In 1919 his first son, Jesse Jr., was born and the Livermores purchased a 29-room mansion in King's Point in Great Neck, Long Island. It became their home. Livermore had a personal barber who shaved him each morning. He was a natty dresser, his suits custom made. So were his shoes. He was 5′10½″ tall, but his shoes contained lifts that elevated him to six feet. He played bridge—Warren Buffett's favorite card game—and enjoyed the shooting sports, housing a large collection of pistols, rifles, and shotguns in his mansion. Dorothy, whom he called "Mousie," gave him a second son, Paul.

Livermore was now at the peak of his career. When Manhattan's then-most glamorous office tower was built in 1921, Livermore took the penthouse for his offices. Then known as the Hecksher Building (now the Crown Building), at 730 Fifth Avenue, between 56th and 57th Streets, the building had an elevator reserved for Livermore. Other guests were seldom permitted on the upper floors. The *New York Times* called Livemore's suite the most palatial in the city, with marble floors and paneled walls. He employed seven men, six chalkboard clerks, and an assistant named Harry Edgar Dacher. Dacher stood six and a half feet tall and weighed nearly three hundred pounds, and protected Livermore's inner office, which was silent as a tomb; he found noise distracting. Even his commute was reported in the newspapers: His chauffeur-driven limousine departed his mansion at 7:20 every morning—he was passionately punctual, very much a creature of routine—and police in New York City green-lighted his car directly to the office. Once a week, Livermore's chauffeur dispensed tips to them, traffic light by traffic light. *Reminiscences* was published; whenever Congress convened hearings on the securities business, Livermore was likely to testify. He amassed one of the largest financial fortunes in the nation in the 1920s, selling out of stocks in the summer of 1929 and beginning a succession of short trades that left him, in the aftermath of the Great Crash, with a fortune of $100 million, every dime of it in cash.

Livermore's life, however, was fragile. His showgirl wife drank heavily and romanced liberally. He fell once more into depression, and it began to dull his trading instincts. He got back into the market on the long side after the crash in what became known as the "suckers' rally." Mousie divorced him in 1932, and she frittered away the millions he did not manage to lose in the market. In 1934 he was forced to declare bankruptcy again. The following year Dorothy shot Jesse Jr. in a drunken argument, leaving the son disabled. Livermore had remarried yet again but he also kept mistresses and his depression increased. Jesse Jr. persuaded him to write his book in the hope it would cheer him up and help him revive his career; he was only 63 years old. With the nation absorbed in the looming war, however, the book did not sell well, and bad reviews did not help—his views were still new and controversial, and the conventional wisdom was against him. On November 27, 1940, he had dinner alone at the Sherry-Netherland Hotel in New York City, went to the lavatory, washed his hands, and shot himself.

The next seminal book Bill Gross picked up as a fresh young PIMCO bond trader was *My Own Story* by Bernard Baruch (Buccaneer Books, 1957). "I've read a number of biographies of Baruch, and actually copied lots of his important quotations relative to the markets," Gross says. The main one of these is the one on his office wall: "Whatever men attempt, they seem driven to try to overdo. When hopes are soaring I always repeat to myself, 'Two and two still make four and no one has ever invented a way of getting something for nothing.' When the outlook is steeped in pessimism I remind myself, 'Two and two make four and you can't keep mankind down for long." Gross says he was impressed with Baruch's "good head" and "common sense."

Bernard Mannes Baruch was born on August 19, 1870, in Camden, South Carolina. His father, Simon, was a German immigrant whose rabbinical family claimed descent from the Bible's Baruch the Scribe. The family had sent 15-year-old Simon to the United States to avoid conscription in the Prussian Army. He was taken under the wing of a former resident of his home village, Mannes Baum, whose first name in gratitude he gave to his son. Baum owned a general store in Camden. Simon was a brilliant student and the Baums sent him to medical school in South Carolina and Virginia. Shortly after he graduated he joined the Confederate Army although, like Robert E. Lee, he owned no slaves and indeed disapproved of slavery; like immigrants before and since, he was showing loyalty to his adopted land. At the Battle of Gettysburg he was taken prisoner; it was one of three times that he was captured by Union forces during the war. Simon Baruch told his son he was treated well as a prisoner of war, and formed a positive view of Yankees, but he was an outspoken critic of Reconstruction, becoming one of the very few Jews to take a prominent role in the infant Ku Klux Klan. He held no enmity for blacks; he treated black and white patients equally. A rising political star, he was elected president of the state medical association and served as head of South Carolina's Board of Health, where he was an advocate for public health systems targeted mainly at the poor. An amateur farmer, the doctor pioneered installing tile drainage systems on low-lying lands, which were disproportionately owned by the poor. Despite his association with the Klan, which he left behind when the family moved to New York City when Bernard was 10, the Baruchs were political liberals. In New York, Simon Baruch became an advocate for the construction of public baths to serve the city's burgeoning tenements. Bernard himself was to make his reputation as an adviser to every Democratic president from Woodrow Wilson to Harry Truman.

Simon Baruch was prosperous but not rich; when the family relocated his net worth was $16,000. Bernard's mother, Isabelle (née Wolfe), however, had come from money. Her father was a slave owner and she told her son that before the Civil War she had never dressed herself. Bernard's grandfather was ruined in the war and Belle, as she was known, found Simon Baruch a good catch when he became the local doctor. She gave him four sons, of whom Bernard was the second.

The ruined economy of the South, particularly under the heel of Reconstruction, offered little to the Baruchs. They decamped to Manhattan in 1880. The city made the same kind of impression on Bernard that San Francisco was to make on Bill Gross, likewise a 10-year-old transplant from a rural area, when he experienced a similar fate nearly 75 years later. Baruch was thrilled by the crowds and the city's abundant and exotic diversions, such as water that flowed out of a tap. "One of the delights of New York is that we did not have to carry water from a well for a bath, as in the South," he wrote in *My Own Story*.

At the age of 14, Bernard enrolled in the City College of New York (CCNY). This was not unusual; there were no public high schools at the time, and his grammar school record was good. He found himself taking a course in what was then called "political economy," in which he was introduced to the law of supply and demand. "Ten years later I was to become rich by remembering those words," he wrote in his autobiography. In New York City, Baruch was first exposed to anti-Semitism. No Jews, himself included, were elected to any of CCNY's numerous fraternities. He said neither he nor his family had ever experienced such prejudice in the South and, indeed, one of his brothers *was* elected to a fraternity at the University of Virginia. In the course of his career Baruch endured unending anti-Semitic attacks.

In college, Baruch displayed a particular aptitude for mathematics, which greatly accelerated his subsequent Wall Street career. He was also an excellent athlete, a wrestler who achieved his adult stature of six feet three inches and 170 pounds while at CCNY. He remained an exercise enthusiast throughout his life.

The Baruchs had intended Bernard for a medical career but he displayed no interest, and became apprenticed instead to a wholesale druggist at three dollars a week. One errand took him into the offices of J. Pierpont Morgan, the nation's dominant financier, and he came away impressed by "his famous nose and tawny eyes. They gave me a feeling of his enormous power." In his leisure time he discovered gambling—to his family's disgust—and after becoming rich would participate in one of the most famous card games ever played, in which John "Bet a Million" Gates, a ruthless industrialist and market speculator, earned his nickname in a private game of baccarat at the Waldorf Hotel. (Other accounts trace the nickname to a bet on a horse, but Gates created a sensation when he bet a million that night.) His famous bet only squared him with the house, and Baruch thought Gates rash. However, as Bill Gross would also discover, Baruch believed gambling and investing called for many of the same skills, including knowing the odds, holding back some cash, and keeping your emotions in check. That famous evening, Baruch's loss was $10,000—exactly what Gross would earn three generations later in Las Vegas, as the first step on his road to fame, wealth, and power.

Baruch's mother, meanwhile, had taken a trip south to visit her family and on the return train was introduced to a German who ran a small investment bank in Manhattan. He was looking for an apprentice, and Bernard soon had the job, although it required a pay cut of three dollars; Julius A. Kohn paid him nothing. But Kohn's firm engaged in arbitrage, the buying of currencies and securities in one marketplace and selling them in another for a small profit. Baruch was able to calculate currency translations and price premiums in his head and on the fly. The firm's account books detailing all of these transactions became, he said, "my favorite reading." His new boss was sufficiently impressed to restore his three-dollar salary.

But Baruch decided what he wanted to do instead was to strike it rich. He and a friend journeyed to Cripple Creek, Colorado, to try their luck in the silver business. Nothing came of it, except that one Cripple Creek saloon had a roulette wheel that Baruch quickly realized was fixed. Whenever sizeable bets were made, they always lost. Baruch began betting against the high rollers, and became so successful he was tossed out. He gave up his mining dreams and returned to Wall Street.

Although Baruch devoted most of his life to public service, investing was his passion. He called the stock market "the total barometer for our civilization." He took a job with a firm called A.A. Houseman & Company and began investing, and losing, small sums. "I began a habit I was never to forsake—of analyzing my losses to determine where I had made my mistakes," he wrote. At the office itself, however, he was the soul of prudence, and Houseman made him a partner at the age of 25. He acquired a Prince Albert coat, a silk hat, and a wife. She was Annie Griffen, whose family were wealthy Episcopalians. He courted her in Central Park, but marriage was slow to come. He was still enamored of the racy life—he was nearly arrested when a cock fight he was attending was raided—and he overplayed his investments. It took him until 1897 to settle down. He bought 100 shares on margin of American Sugar Refining, which controlled three-quarters of its marketplace and paid high dividends. It was embroiled in a fight over tariffs in Congress. Baruch reasoned that the company would win the fight. It did, and as Baruch's profits had increased he had reinvested them, giving him a total gain of $60,000. He married Annie—over the strong objections of her family, owing to their different religions—in 1897 and bought a seat on the New York Stock Exchange to engage in speculation full time.

As with Jesse Livermore, "speculator" was a word Baruch wore proudly. Despite the tarnish it had acquired throughout the nineteenth century, when stock raiders were just as happy to destroy companies as profit from them, the classically educated Baruch noted that the word derived from the Latin *speculari*, which means to observe. He had established three rules he was to follow scrupulously: first, to get all the facts on a potential investment, then to make what he called an informed judgment about that information, and finally to act promptly—"before it is too late," he wrote.

He confirmed the final of these tenets in what he called his "first big deal," a huge rally that followed the United States' 1898 success against Spain in that year's war between the two nations. Baruch got wind on Sunday, July 3, of a crucial victory in Santiago Bay, Chile. U.S. markets would be closed the following day but European markets were open. Like most of Wall Street, Baruch was vacationing on the New Jersey shore. (The Hamptons had not become popular yet.) The news came late at night, and no trains to Manhattan could be found. So Baruch hired one. He knew the story of how the Rothschilds had made their fortune using carrier pigeons to bring news of the Battle of Waterloo ahead of everyone else, and jumped on the 1898 equivalent. The Houseman firm spent the night buying U.S. shares in London. It benefited hugely, and its reputation (especially Baruch's) spread.

In 1901, Baruch made his first killing—a profit of $700,000—on the short sale of stock in Amalgamated Copper Company. Insiders and promoters sent the stock flying to $130 a share. In reality, world copper demand was being choked off by the high prices that supported the stock rise. Baruch saw what he called "the irresistible force of economic gravitation" about to play out. Although close friends told him he was being played a fool, he stuck to his guns. He eventually rode the shares down to $60, and further cemented his reputation. Woodrow Wilson, who made Baruch a close adviser, called him "Mr. Facts."

But it was in panics that Baruch's most valuable insight—that facts remain facts even when emotions are high—was forged. He made fortunes in the panics of 1901 and 1907 because he had sold short into the debacles and went long afterward. "During a depression people come to feel that better times never will come," he wrote in his auto-biography. "At such times a basic confidence in the country's future pays off, if one purchases securities and holds them until prosperity returns."

Baruch continued to enjoy a series of coups. In 1901 he scored a home run in rubber after acquiring his first automobile and learning that tires lasted only a few hundred miles. In his autobiography, he drolly notes that the machine came with a chauffeur whom he was forced to discharge. "Heinrich was a good man when sober," Baruch wrote. "But his delinquencies added too much to an already zestful sport." In 1902, he bettered J. Pierpont Morgan himself in a fight over control of the Louisville & Nashville Railroad, emerging not with the road—Baruch said his greatest disappointment in life was never owning a railroad—but with $1 million he maneuvered out of Morgan. By the age of 32, he calculated, he had amassed $100,000 for every year of his life. In the Panic of 1907 he personally pledged $1.5 million to Morgan's lending pool, reportedly the largest single commitment next to Pierpont's. Two years later Morgan asked him to evaluate a sulfur mine in Texas. He was so impressed that he told Morgan he would be willing to "gamble" half the $500,000 price tag himself. "'I never gamble,' replied Mr. Morgan with a gesture that signified the interview was over," he later wrote. In the First World War, sulfur became so valuable that Baruch's fortune exploded. Pierpont had died in 1913 and the Morgan firm came into Baruch's deal, and just the small share he apportioned to the firm became worth $70 million. (Except that the firm had flipped the deal at a small profit to someone else, not giving Baruch the opportunity to buy it back, which he greatly resented.)

Baruch had become a contributor to Democratic politicians, and was soon regarded as the party's financier in New York and, ultimately, the nation. He became an adviser to Woodrow Wilson in 1916 and was later named head of his War Industries Board. He attended the Versailles Peace Conference as Wilson's personal adviser. He began suffering anti-Semitic attacks from Father Charles F. Coughlin, the Ku Klux Klan, and Henry Ford, who in the Dearborn (Michigan) *Independent* labeled Baruch a member of the "international Jewish conspiracy." He continued to invest, but less actively than before. In 1929, like Livermore and Joe Kennedy, he sold the market short well ahead of the crash, and three years later, like them, was hauled before Congress under suspicion of engineering the debacle. For one thing, Baruch was a Jew and Kennedy a Roman Catholic, and they achieved their social prominence over the snide opposition of Wall Street's WASP establishment, the House of Morgan foremost among that group. The "bear hunt" was purely political, however, and in 1934 Franklin Delano Roosevelt named Kennedy as the first chairman of the new Securities & Exchange Commission, and employed Baruch as a personal adviser. He was part of the team that created the United Nations. During the Truman and Kennedy administrations he was regarded as an "elder statesman." Baruch died in 1965 at the age of 95 in Manhattan, where today Baruch College is part of the City University System. In South Carolina, the Belle W. Baruch Institute, established in honor of his mother, supports environmental research.

Bill Gross had been introduced to J.P. Morgan's ideas in business school, and what struck him was the famous banker's rectitude. The quote he has put on his office wall is this: "Lending is not based primarily upon money or property. No sir. The first thing is character." While I was interviewing Gross for this book, he remarked: "In the last few years we've seen what the character of many of our larger corporations has become. Enron. Worldcom." What also impressed him about the great banker was his decisiveness. "He was forceful at the appropriate time and was willing to take measured risk," Gross says. "Measured" is a carefully chosen word. Unlike Livermore and Baruch, Morgan was anything but a speculator.

To John Pierpont Morgan, Livermore and Baruch, whom he knew, although only slightly, were children—literally. His own son J.P. Jr., called Jack, was born in 1867, three years before Baruch and ten years before Livermore. Whereas Livermore was born into a hardscrabble life and Baruch's family was only prosperous, Morgan's was both rich and important. When Bill Gross's other two investment heroes were still in short pants, Morgan's father was establishing himself as one of the most important financiers on the planet, and his son was doing the same on his native soil, which he helped make the most important on the planet. The other two are the lesser figures in the Gross Trinity. Morgan is first, in memory as he was in life. The virtue he displayed was also core rather than tertiary—in Gross's terminology, secular as opposed to cyclical. Gross's quote is drawn from testimony Pierpont gave to Congress in which he implicitly rebuked his interrogators who insinuated that bankers lent only on the basis of crass commercial considerations. Historians divide themselves into those who believe men makes the times and those who think times make men. What history records as the era of "manifest destiny" found full expression in the considerable person of J. Pierpont Morgan. In his time, the most common motto on college campuses was *carpe diem*— seize the day. Pierpont seized an era.

J.P. Morgan was born on April 17, 1837, in Hartford, Connecticut. His father, Junius Spencer Morgan, was a banker and a merchant; merchant, or investment, banking had its source in commercial letters of credit. Junius's father, Joseph Morgan, was also a banker who carefully guided his son's career. His mother, Juliet Pierpont, was from a venerable Yankee family of preachers and poets, one of whom wrote "Jingle Bells." Pierpont was sickly, and would remain so throughout his 75 years of life. He inherited from his mother's side a congenital skin disease, rosacea, which in his middle years distorted his nose into a venous purplish lump that frightened children. When Edward Steichen took his famous portrait photograph, Pierpont refused to sit for a profile, staring balefully into the camera head-on for two minutes and then leaving. His name was nearly as ponderous as his nose, and he was called by a variety of childish nicknames until, when he learned to write, he wrote his signature as J. Pierpont Morgan. His friends and family called him Pierpont ever after. Even when his partners were included, this was never a large number of people: Everyone else called him Mr. Morgan.

What would become the House of Morgan was evolving in London, years before, where George Peabody, a merchant from Baltimore, had opened a bank to help direct British investments into the most promising American ventures. London was the financial center of the day and the United States was a burgeoning marketplace that needed capital for its river-borne commerce. Junius Morgan became Peabody's partner in 1854; when Morgan's father had died a few years earlier, he had left an estate of more than $1 million. Peabody's firm would eventually become J.S. Morgan and Company. Junius would spend most of his life in London, with Pierpont eventually taking over the New York operations. In the son's lifetime, America's subservient financial relationship with Great Britain would be reversed, with Pierpont playing the dominant role in this transformation.

Pierpont enjoyed an unremarkable education, studying indifferently before taking an apprenticeship in Manhattan at the age of 20 with Peabody's U.S. agent, Duncan, Sherman & Company. (Jack Morgan was the first in his family to graduate from college.) The Panic of 1857 was Pierpont's introduction to the woeful state of American finance. There was no central bank, the populist Andrew Jackson having dissolved it a generation earlier. States and even private banks issued their own currencies. The Peabody firm dealt mainly in the bonds of states and their public works, such as canals. The role of the federal government in fostering and regulating the national economy would remain rudimentary for most of Pierpont's life, and indeed it was the vacuum in American financial leadership that Pierpont was to fill.

Peabody was old and Junius Morgan took over the firm in 1859. It played only a minor role in financing the Civil War, as most of these bonds were underwritten by New York's Jewish firms, such as Kuhn Loeb, which had historic links with German financiers, who were strongly pro-Union. Pierpont did manage one small deal in those years, however, cabling his father with early news of the North's victory at Vicksburg in 1863 and allowing the elder Morgan to snap up American bonds in London before the news became public, and thus to benefit when they rallied. When Peabody died in 1869, Pierpont arranged his funeral. He was Junius's sole surviving son, and nineteenth century merchant banks were family affairs; it was inconceivable that Pierpont would follow another career. This was also true of his son, Jack, who had wanted to be a doctor but was condemned to join the family firm by what Ron Chernow, in *The House of Morgan* (Simon & Schuster, 1990) calls the "Gentleman Banker's Code."

Pierpont was a conventional and even archetypal WASP: white, Yankee, Episcopalian. He was deeply religious and adhered to a strong moral code; his word was always his bond, and all his deals were concluded with handshakes. He pursued art collecting and philanthropy with as much attention as he gave to work, which was considerable. At the same time, however, he was dangerously romantic. His first marriage was to Amelia Sturgis, who was dying of tuberculosis when he married her and perished on their honeymoon. Her name was considered sacred in his household, and he venerated her memory tenderly. She was his one true love and his more enduring marriage, in 1865 to Francis Louisa Tracy, whom he called Fanny, was ultimately hollow. Morgan's famous yachts were as much pleasure barges as anything else, and he indulged in constant affairs at home and in Europe.

When Junius ruled the firm from London, he was vying principally with the two established merchant banking families of the time, the Rothschilds and the Barings. In 1870, when France was under attack by Prussia, it sought financing in London, and turned to Morgan. Barings was aligned with Prussia and the Rothschilds abstained, assuming France would lose. Morgan organized a syndicate that, while it extracted harsh terms from the French, nevertheless floated the bonds. Junius risked his own fortune when military reversals sent the bonds down and he bought them to support their price. France lost the war but did not repudiate the bonds, restoring their price to par and delivering a genuine fortune to Morgan. The deal also made his reputation.

Back at home, Pierpont had grown into an imposing man: more than six feet tall and stocky, with penetrating hazel eyes. He always dressed formally, wearing different hats according to the season and sometimes sporting checkered vests. He was making a reputation for himself of dealing fair—and strong. His most important early deal, in 1869, turned on a small New York railroad that was being fought over by Jay Gould and Joseph Ramsey. Pierpont was hired by Ramsey to wrest back control of his road from the raider. Morgan hatched a bold scheme. He located an upstate judge who ousted the Gould forces from the railroad's board, and meanwhile arranged for a friendly merger of the line with a larger, raid-proof road. In addition to his fee, he extracted from the deal a seat on the board of the merged road. Although he remained a banker throughout his life, and represented what came to be known as the Money Trust, he was likewise a powerful businessman, a robber baron of that Gilded Age. He never amassed the huge fortune of Andrew Carnegie or John D. Rockefeller but he had more power than either of them. More power, in fact, than anyone in that headstrong era, as he was to demonstrate to President Theodore Roosevelt in the Panic of 1907, the resolution of which was to become his climactic achievement.

Junius had arranged, meanwhile, for an important Philadelphia banker, Tony Drexel, to form a partnership with his son. The Drexels could see that New York was supplanting their native city as the United States' financial center, and the firm of Drexel, Morgan, and Company was formed in 1871 to unite the two families. (It would remain Drexel Morgan until 1910, when it became J.P. Morgan and Company.) Two years later the firm established its headquarters at 23 Wall Street, on the opposite corner of Broad Street from the New York Stock Exchange. Also that year, Pierpont also helped engineer a seismic shift in his firm's importance when it led a syndicate that captured half of $300 million refunding of the nation's Civil War debt.

The entire deal would otherwise have gone to Jay Cooke, Drexel's chief financial rival in Philadelphia. J.S. Morgan and Company as well as Barings also participated in Pierpont's syndicate, the first time the son delivered a substantial financial prize to his father, rather than the reverse. To ice the cake, Cooke's empire crumbled that same year, precipitating the Panic of 1873. European railroad investors, in particular, were wiped out. But Pierpont had not speculated in railroad shares and emerged from the debacle with a profit of $1 million. In addition, the Drexel Morgan firm emerged as a pillar of rectitude, and never in Pierpont's lifetime did it lose a scintilla of its accreting power.

Pierpont had always been warned by his father against stock speculation, and the Panic of 1873 cemented Pierpont's oligarchical view of American finance. This emblem of capitalism detested competition and did his best to eliminate it at every turn. He acted in the name and interest of his bondholders; in those days, merchant bankers were personally responsible for the actions of their houses, and either thrived or were ruined with them. To the degree possible, Pierpont daringly engineered financial deals that involved the least possible risk to bondholders. This lead to trusts—giant conglomerates of natural competitors who united to conspire against their marketplaces. More than anyone of his era, even Rockefeller, Pierpont exploited trusts to create and exploit monopolies. He engineered the creation of the General Electric Company and, his biggest deal, the United States Steel Corporation, the first billion-dollar company, immediately accounting for one-ninth of the total capitalization of the entire U.S. stock market. In the case of U.S. Steel he paid without a quibble Andrew Carnegie's demand of $480 million for his industrial empire, making Carnegie the richest American of the day. Carnegie boasted, in reference to himself as well as to Morgan's ascension over Wall Street's older merchant banks, "It takes a Yankee to beat a Jew, and it takes a Scot to beat a Yankee!" In fact, Pierpont valued Carnegie's holdings $100 million higher than the steel magnate did, which Carnegie later was ruefully to acknowledge was probably true.

With the death of his father in 1890, Pierpont became the lead partner in all of the family's partnerships, which included other firms in Europe. He was a demanding taskmaster, working himself and his partners mercilessly; the House of Morgan became infamous for the number of its partners who died young, including those who died by their own hand. He was not naturally drawn to arduous work; his health was always fragile. He was known for snap decisions rather than endless analysis; he took no longer to accept Carnegie's asking price than it took to read the number the Scot had penciled on a scrap of paper. To compensate for 16-hour days at the office, Pierpont took lengthy vacations, usually three months and usually on one of his yachts, all named *Corsair*. He liked to hint that he was descended from the pirate Henry Morgan. The biggest of these vessels was more than 300 feet long and would have been bigger except it had to be able to turn around in the Hudson River near Morgan's summer home in Cragston. Many of Morgan's most famous deals, including the vast network of railroads he assumed control of in the 1880s and 1890s, were hammered out on the yacht. The others were done most often at his sumptuous library in Manhattan's Murray Hill neighborhood, which still stands as a now-public institution. Manhattan is dotted with vestiges of his presence; he was a principal patron of the Metropolitan Museum of Art, the American Museum of Natural History, and the Metropolitan Opera. The building that housed the original headquarters of his firm remains on Wall Street, just a few paces from the grave in Trinity Churchyard of Alexander Hamilton.

As the twentieth century began, Morgan spent more and more time traveling. His wife had long since ceased to accompany him on these expeditions—he visited Egypt three times in his last three years of life—and he was increasingly rumored to have clandestine liaisons with socially prominent women in Europe and New York. Theodore Roosevelt, who became president when William McKinley was assassinated, was much less friendly to trusts than his predecessor had been. He began waging war with the House of Morgan, which

Pierpont generally ignored or left to his lieutenants (one of whom was his grown son, Jack). When the Panic of 1907 erupted, Pierpont was in Richmond, Virginia, as a lay delegate at the Episcopal Convention. The Panic was potentially the worst of Morgan's lifetime and, recognizing his public responsibility, he rushed to New York to personally manage the disaster.

The year 1907 was full both of calamity and rampant stock speculation. The Egyptian Stock Exchange collapsed. So did the exchange in Tokyo, taking Japan's banks with it. The Bank of England ran short of reserves. Bonds of Boston and New York City sold poorly; San Francisco, desperate to rebuild after the prior year's earthquake, could not borrow at all. Major corporations went bankrupt. When the U.S. stock market crashed on Aug. 10, losses were pegged at a record $1 billion. Wall Street blamed Theodore Roosevelt's trust busting, which was eroding business confidence. Roosevelt blamed a conspiracy of Wall Street titans—"certain malefactors of great wealth," as he called them, reportedly staring down at Pierpont Morgan, a guest at the speech, as he said those words. Then in the autumn rural banks, as they did every year, drained capital out of New York to settle the season's harvests. In October, the Knickerbocker Trust failed after paying out $8 million in a run by depositors.

Upon his return to the city, Pierpont had organized a committee of bankers to help him deal with the crisis, and when it audited Knickerbocker, Pierpont concluded it could not be saved. Instead he decided to defend a stronger firm, Trust Company of America. Throughout the month of October Morgan, aided by New York's top commercial bankers and with a pledge of $25 million from the federal government, labored to stanch the run on the trusts, and then the banks. On October 24, the Panic spilled over on the New York Stock Exchange as call money, or brokers' loans to support margin, evaporated. The exchange's president called on Morgan for help, and within 15 minutes he had lined up a further $25 million in credit to support the call money market. When that news was announced on the floor of the exchange, traders celebrated so wildly that Morgan could hear them in his office.

The Panic was not over. Having saved virtually the entire banking and brokerage industries from ruin, Morgan turned to the city of New York, whose finances had been thrown into a shambles by the panic. Unable to borrow money, the city's mayor called on Morgan for a $30 million loan and got it. And then Morgan concentrated on himself. In a complicated series of maneuvers, he agreed to shore up a weak brokerage firm that had a claim on controlling interest in Tennessee Coal and Iron Company. Literally locking the bankers, trust officers, and industrial magnates inside his library all night to come to terms, Pierpont emerged with control of Tennessee Coal, which he promptly added to U.S. Steel's diadem of industrial jewels. The deal could never have been done in ordinary circumstances, since it patently violated the Sherman Antitrust Act, legislation that Roosevelt was enforcing with enthusiasm. But Roosevelt was forced to accept the deal in the interest of ending the panic, and signed off to two Morgan emissaries who had been dispatched by overnight train to Washington to get his signature.

With the panic ended, Morgan returned to semi-retirement, working only a few hours here and there, devoting himself mostly to his collections, including an art collection that was regarded as the finest in private hands in the nation. One of his trusts had built the *Titanic*, and he had a personal suite aboard, which he visited before the ship's maiden voyage. But he cancelled his reservation for the initial voyage and learned about the great ship's sinking in April 1912 while traveling in France. Almost immediately he was hauled before Congress, which used the sinking as a lever to attack the trust that had built it and the man who had created the trust. Morgan for most of his life had been unpopular among debtors, which most Americans were: When William Jennings Bryan thundered about a "cross of gold," he was talking about Morgan, who in 1895 had maneuvered to hold the United States to the gold standard. Morgan was treated harshly by the House Banking and Currency Committee, but it elicited the quote Bill Gross has on his office wall. As quoted in the Congressional Record, the exchange between Morgan and Samuel Untermyer, the committee's legal counsel, went in full like this:

> Untermyer: *Is not commercial credit based primarily upon money or property?*
>
> Morgan: *No, sir; the first thing is character.*
>
> Untermyer: *Before money or property?*
>
> Morgan: *Before money or property or anything else. Money cannot buy it.....A man I do not trust could not get money from me on all the bonds in Christendom.*

Pierpont Morgan was physically exhausted by the hearings, and returned almost at once to Europe to recuperate. In a lavish suite in a Rome hotel, he died at night on March 31, 1913, at the age of 75. His daughter Louisa was with him; she reported to her brother that their father had surrendered control of the House of Morgan to him. When his obituary was published in the *New York Times*, it estimated his fortune at $100 million. When he read it, Carnegie exclaimed, "And to think he was not a rich man!"

The year Morgan died the United States created the Federal Reserve System, and the nation's central banking power was never left in an individual's hands again. But the House of Morgan continued to play a vital role in the nation's finances for the balance of the twentieth century. The firm was, in the end, Pierpont's most important achievement. He transformed a middling offshore bank into the most powerful financial institution in the world. He cultivated partners and gave them so much authority that his passing left the firm undamaged. Although he was dominating and even imperious in his prime, his greatest talent was in his vision and his ability to marshal resources to express it, not in the management of the resulting enterprise. He left it to the industrialists he recruited to run his trusts. He left details like contracts to his subordinates. He was consistently close-mouthed; above his desk he kept a plaque with the legend, *Pense moult, Parle peu, Écris rien*. (Think a lot, Say little, Write nothing.) Yet the man who complained repeatedly that he was unable to delegate authority managed to do so, very successfully.

Gross applied lessons from the lives of Baruch, Morgan, and Livermore to his own, using them (as well as Ed Thorpe's "Beat The Market" system) as cornerstones of his investment philosophy.

Gross found confirmation in Jesse Livermore's life for his sense that number patterns, discernable to only the talented few, can be used to reap financial rewards. He discovered yet again the costs that come from allowing emotions and whims to govern investment decisions, and the strictness and rigor, even asceticism, required of those who use a particular system to make money in the markets. If Livermore had "stuck to his knitting," he would have died a wealthier and happier man.

Baruch's work affirmed Gross's belief that investing is, indeed, akin to gambling—but with much better odds. Baruch's success came from investing for the long term, refusing to act during short-term panics or crazes, and from applying all of the available information on the world economy and international business to the financial markets. Gross's zeal for discovering mispricings, seeking advice from experts, predicting the cyclical moods of the world's economies, and using these predictions to make money from bonds echo Baruch's skills and practices.

While Livermore and Baruch inspired Gross to reach conclusions about the nature of markets and investing, Morgan's life became a template for Bill's mission to found a successful investment company. Since the beginning of his career, Bill Gross has had his eye on building an investment organization that would be bigger than himself. He has always delegated to his partners the tasks he did not feel up to himself, such as day-to-day management and client relations. He has created a process, based on the firm's famous Secular Forums, that involves every professional employee in informed decision making. The firm's investment stance is dictated not by Gross personally, but by his Investment Committee. Even non-partners have appeared before the Committee and defended investment decisions with which Gross disagreed. Autocracy is less fashionable in 2004 than it was in 1904, but investment firms that rely on a single individual are no more likely now than then to survive. Using the examples of Morgan and Drexel, Gross and his partners have built PIMCO into an investment organization likely to be around long after they have retired to their collections and philanthropies.

PART TWO

Total Return Investing

CHAPTER 4

A Waterlogged World

At the foundation of Bill Gross's investment approach is a long-term framework for anticipating change in securities markets. Three of the investors he has modeled himself after—Livermore, Baruch and Ed Thorpe—were distinguished by their ability to grasp trends and their implications more quickly than their rivals. Livermore could see patterns in the movement of numbers on the ticker tapes of Boston bucket shops; Baruch could see the big picture, the ebbs and flows in securities prices, despite whatever craze or panic was going on around him; Thorpe had an uncanny eye for inaccurate pricing of illiquid investments (in his case, convertible bonds) and the ability to take advantage of it. Gross's other mentor (in a competitive, contemporary way), Warren Buffett, is able to foresee changes in the economy and the markets that would transform life and present investing opportunities. This keen predictive ability lies at the heart of Gross's decision to design and implement PIMCO's secular forums.

Early in his career Gross felt, and still does, that understanding the basis of change in the marketplace acts as a control on emotion; he strives not to be taken by surprise, but rather to view change as just one more market dynamic that can be studied and managed. Gross studies change over two quite distinct time horizons. As we've explored, the shorter of the two, with a range of three to 12 months, he calls "cyclical," and the longer, with a range of three to five years, "secular." (His language is that of economics, not religion.)

Since shortly after Gross began implementing his total-return investment approach in the early 1970s, PIMCO has devoted itself to anticipating change through a structure of "step-back" seminars intended to take Gross and his portfolio managers away from their desks in order to take a hard look at events and to attempt to tease out their implications. From 1975 to 1981, these consisted of quarterly meetings of the investment team focused on cyclical change. Yet, by definition, these meetings were reactive rather than mechanisms for honing foresight. Cyclical changes, such as the Russian default of 1998, the Swedish vote on the euro of 2003, or the result of the 2000 U.S. Presidential election, are almost impossible to forecast with any degree of success. Attempting to anticipate them is rather like casting runes or reading tea leaves. Who could have anticipated the assassination of Swedish minister Anna Lindh, and this event's failure to alter Sweden's rejection of the euro in a national referendum a few days later? Or, for that matter, the extraordinary events of *Bush v. Gore*? While it is of critical importance for investors to react to rapidly changing world events by altering their portfolios to take advantage of them, it is a way to save money and cut losses, not a way to proactively make money.

By 1982, however, Gross felt a secular forum was needed to develop a broader context for investment decisions. That year the firm's first Secular Forum was held. Two outside speakers were invited to address PIMCO's managers: Charles Maxwell, the noted energy analyst, to explore the broad trends affecting that sector, and economist

John Rutledge to analyze macroeconomic and financial trends. Secular Forums have been held annually since, supplementing quarterly Cyclical Forums, and as they have evolved their agenda has expanded to the point that today's forums feature five or six speakers on an equally expansive range of topics.

"We don't simply focus on economics," Gross explains. "We try to bring in demographics, politics and other areas that will impact the long-run secular outlook." Over the years, speakers have included former or about-to-be-appointed governors of the Federal Reserve System, like Wayne Angell and Ben Barnanke. Heavyweight investment bankers like Henry Kaufman, and Wall Street gurus like Stephen Roach of Morgan Stanley, are routinely invited. Prominent market researchers like Steve Leuthold and Jeremy Grantham have appeared. So have political and social commentators. Zbigniew Brzezinski addressed the group after leaving Jimmy Carter's administration; Robert Reich spoke before joining Bill Clinton's. Walter Rostow, the Kennedy-Johnson–era Cold Warrior, addressed the forum in 1986, just when the Cold War was sputtering out. Social critics like Kevin Phillips and William Greider appear frequently; both of these men addressed the forum in 2003. In 2002, historian Jonathan Spence of Yale University discoursed on the development of modern China. Guillermo Calvo, director of the Center for International Economics at the University of Maryland, appeared at PIMCO's 1995 forum to address the Mexican debt crisis of the prior year and its implications throughout Latin America. In 1998, the chief economist for the Americas of UBS Warburg, Paul McCulley, so impressed Gross and his partners that he was soon invited to rejoin the firm, which he had left six years earlier, and is now PIMCO's Fed watcher and manager of short-duration portfolios.

Gross invites the speakers and thus sets the agenda for the forums. (McCulley does the same for the quarterly cyclical conclaves.) The ideas to be explored have arisen throughout the preceding year; its most nettlesome investment dilemmas are grist for the forum's mill.

PIMCO's staff prepares briefing documents that include hundreds of pages of research related to that year's topics: For 2003's meeting, they included demographics, productivity, inflation and monetary policy, fiscal policy, relative asset returns, international trade, and the Chinese marketplace. Other preparatory materials include readings suggested by the speakers. After their remarks, speakers are questioned at length, and equally lengthy discussions among the staff follow. The meetings are held around a vast conference table in a lecture hall at PIMCO's headquarters. The hall seats about 100 people; the balance participate by closed-circuit television from smaller conference rooms throughout the headquarters complex.

PIMCO's current investment stance grew out of the 2003 Secular Forum, which was held in May in Newport Beach. Although outsiders are not allowed to attend the meeting, I was invited to sit in on your behalf.

Many of the recommendations Bill Gross makes in these pages grew out of the Forum. This three-day session brought into focus several trends that subsequently became front-page news during the year, notably the parlous state of the nation's pension industry. "We discuss and sift and don't necessarily agree," Gross says, "but we do come to a conclusion, and we do act on that conclusion." As often as every business day when PIMCO's Investment Committee meets, alternative investment decisions are discussed in the context of the firm's secular outlook. The forum leads, Gross says, "to an investment strategy that we fairly consistently employ over the next 12 months."

When the PIMCO team met, it was managing more than $330 billion on behalf of individual and institutional investors. It was the most respected fixed-income management firm because it was the most successful. Gross attributes this in part to the firm's long-range view. Many if not most professional investors are overly immersed in the myriad details of markets day to day. PIMCO ignores much of this as meaningless "noise," or seeks to exploit inefficiencies it creates. Hewing to a discipline based on thoroughly understanding long-term trends in society and world affairs allows PIMCO's managers and traders to brace themselves against emotions of the moment.

The theme of 2003's conference was captured in one of Gross's folksy metaphors: "How Wet are the Logs?" "Wet logs" is the name given to the developed world's economies mired in or close to recession: They are not igniting easily. U.S. interest rates at the time of the forum were about to fall to 1 percent, their lowest level in nearly 50 years. Low rates are a prime lever in engineering economic recovery. They encourage consumers to borrow and spend, and push corporations to borrow and invest. Interest rates in Japan were already effectively zero. The European Central Bank would shortly lower rates as well, to combat frailty in its own economies. This stimulus, however, was not working as it always had before.

The fundamental issue was jobs. In the late 1990s, PIMCO's forums helped it identify a trend that has subsequently become obvious: China (and now, to a lesser degree, India) is exporting wage deflation to the rest of the world. The profound changes this has led to was America's economic quandary—how could the economy be in recovery when jobs were continuing to disappear? One of 2003's speakers was Martin Feldstein, who is chief executive officer of the National Bureau of Economic Research (NBER). This is the official arbiter of the U.S. business cycle. Feldstein, who was also an economic adviser to Ronald Reagan, is George F. Baker Professor of Economics at Harvard. The NBER, which is headquartered in Boston, determines (often long after the fact) when the United States enters, and then recovers from, recession. Unofficially, recession is usually described as two or more fiscal quarters of negative growth of gross domestic product, or GDP, and recovery as two consecutive positive quarters. But the Bureau's definition is much more focused on employment than GDP, as Feldstein explained to the forum participants, and the disparity between the two gauges was sharply drawn in the spring of 2003. The nation at the time had produced four consecutive quarters of GDP growth, albeit feeble, and many pundits were therefore declaring the recession over. But unemployment remained stubbornly high. The Bureau, therefore, had not put its imprimatur on recovery. When it did, declaring in July 2003 that the recession that began in March 2001 had ended just eight months later, employment remained the hottest domestic economic topic. Government data showed that between November 2001, which the NBER dated as the beginning of recovery, and the first quarter of 2003, employers shed more than 900,000 jobs. Additionally, more than 150,000 job seekers had abandoned their search. Indeed, the NBER said when it announced its decision in July that it had had to bend its own employment-heavy weighting system to declare recovery under way.

China's current role in the world economic order is to act as a mammoth factory—an outsource for the developed world's manufacturers. So inexpensive is the Chinese work force that even Mexico and South Korea are losing manufacturing jobs to it. And China is not exporting wage deflation only—it is also exporting price deflation in its finished goods. At the time PIMCO's managers were meeting, the Federal Reserve was radically altering its own secular vision of its responsibility as a central bank. For a generation it had been aggressively, consistently, and successfully focused on bringing down inflation; at the time of the meeting, the U.S. consumer price index was rising at a 2.8 percent rate, down from double digits 20 years earlier. Guarding against inflation is the traditional role of central bankers. But the Fed was deciding, and would subsequently announce, that it was switching to a new policy focus: fighting deflation. The implication of such a policy shift is support for rising, rather than falling, prices—that is, inflation—and the impact of that on bonds is bad. Bondholders' goal is to preserve their purchasing power. In the course of the 2003 forum, Gross and his team were deciding to adopt a more conservative approach to managing portfolios, such as shorting average duration in anticipation of higher rates. In fact, this occurred with unexpected swiftness only two months later, when long-term interest rates ballooned as the market absorbed the Fed's meaning.

The role of China in global economic affairs was also starkly evident in the fact that PIMCO's Asian managers, who ordinarily would have been attending the forum, were absent because of the SARS threat. Sudden acute respiratory syndrome, which had originated in China the previous autumn and then spread to Hong Kong and elsewhere, was new. Little was known about it except that it was often lethal. An emerging global economic recovery in late 2002 had been damped down by the SARS virus; the subsequent rise in U.S. rates was so explosive because domestic economic activity was hurt by the fallout much less than had been feared. In addition, the release of stronger-than-expected economic numbers in June and July, combined with the Fed's new focus, caused massive selling of U.S. Treasury bonds and of mortgage-backed securities, which are also hyper-sensitive to rates. SARS was, therefore, on the forum's agenda as well, and although bond markets were extremely strong at the time the meeting was held, one of its conclusions was to begin reining in portfolio duration.

Gross had introduced this notion in his opening remarks to the forum. "Wet logs" suggest very slow growth, impeded by the inability of governments to stimulate their economies and the unwillingness or inability of corporations to hire and spend. Slow growth means corporate earnings will not accelerate as much as they typically do in an economic recovery. It means inflation will remain negligible; indeed, deflation is the more immediate concern (as the Fed would formally acknowledge within weeks). So the meeting would explore, Gross said, whether the world had enough tinder to ignite the soaked economic logs. It failed spectacularly to do so in the 1930s, and future failures are not impossible. Alan Greenspan has enjoyed an unusually long and successful reign as chairman of the Federal Reserve because of his adroit manipulation of economic levers, but deflation (also the cause of the Great Depression) is what PIMCO's McCulley has described as "the burden the beast of capitalism cannot bear." As Japan's lamentable experience proves, only aggressive efforts by governments can unwind its economic tentacles.

Gross posed three fundamental questions that he said the forum was intended to answer:

1. "Shall we keep the carry?"
2. "Shall we go to cash and give up the carry?"
3. "Or shall we keep on eating salad?"

In a sense, the bond business is all about cash and carry, or more accurately, cash versus carry. *Carry* is financial jargon for the premium that bonds pay for accepting risk. Long Treasuries offer carry above the coupons of short issues. Corporates have more carry than Treasuries, and high-yield corporates more still. When Gross referred to "cash" he did not mean the bills in the wallets of professional investors—he referred to money represented by very short-term money market instruments, such as overnight bank and corporate loans. Going to cash is what investment managers do when they cannot do anything else, when they cannot find carry in the markets worth paying for. It is an extremely defensive measure, and an expensive one. Returns on cash substitutes like commercial paper in the spring of 2003 were at decades-old lows, little more than the cost of servicing the portfolio. "Eating salad" is a reference to Gross's description of the great bond bull market of the 1980s and 1990s as the salad days for fixed-income investors: yields were lush, risks were low, and prices steadily appreciated. Treasury bonds were the greatest beneficiaries of those trends because the only risk to which they are vulnerable is the risk of rising interest rates. "Eating salad" means harvesting lush returns from the highest-quality debt—something the forum's agenda was already calling into question.

Having set the stage, Gross turned the meeting over to Kevin Phillips. Phillips came to prominence in the late 1960s with the publication of his book, *The Emerging Republican Majority* (Arlington House, 1969). He was editor and publisher of *The American Political Report*, and also wrote *The Politics of Rich and Poor* (Random House,

1990) and, more recently, *Wealth and Democracy* (Broadway Books, 2002). Phillips had distributed a paper to the forum's attendees titled "Hegemony, Hubris and Overreach." He launched immediately into a blistering analysis of United States foreign and economic policy. He compared the United States' invasion of Afghanistan and Iraq to the military adventures of Spain, Holland, and Great Britain when they were at the height of their power. These are clear examples of over-reach, he said, concluding the United States is equally vulnerable now. American hubris, he argued, is a symptom not of power, but of decline. Gross had already been converted to this view: In his March 2003 "Investment Outlook" he announced, to a fury documented in the *Wall Street Journal*, his opposition to the invasion of Iraq.

Another of Phillips's papers submitted to conference partici-pants was called "How Wealth Defines Power: The Politics of a New Gilded Age." In his talk, Phillips wove those ideas into those of over-reach. To him, the high-tech frenzy of the late 1990s was eerily similar to what Mark Twain dubbed the "Gilded Age" 100 years earlier. Those who speak of a "New Paradigm" in our era have forgotten that such utopias have been proclaimed before: In the 1920s, the famed economist Irving Fisher said the nation had achieved a "permanent platform of prosperity."

Phillips cited reams of data showing rapid concentration of wealth in the hands of relatively few—exactly what occurred in the Gilded Age. Before the Civil War broke out, the largest fortune in the country was Commodore Vanderbilt's $15 million. By 1900, Andrew Carnegie and John D. Rockefeller were worth more than $300 million each, and inflation over those 40 years was negligible; the gains were real. In 1980, the average compensation of the 10 most highly paid corporate chieftains was $3.5 million. In 2000, it was $155 million. "No previous era matches this," Phillips said.

The difference between the eras of the Gilded Age and the New Paradigm, however, is that the United States was not a world power a century ago, and now it is *the* world power. The consequences of its actions are correspondingly magnified. He warned ominously that the United States is being "Japanized"—that is, hollowed out of its core economic virtues and left a fragile financial shell. The United States' current-account deficit is 5 percent of gross domestic product; when Britain labored under a 6 percent deficit early in the twentieth century, its economy was crushed.

Phillips's analysis directly challenged one of PIMCO's secular themes, which is enthusiasm for globalization. The "hollowing out" of the nation's manufacturing sector was already fueling the fires of anti-globalization. A growing current-account deficit is also bad for the dollar—which was losing value against the euro and yen as the meeting was held—and that would reverberate throughout the world of fixed-income securities. In response to a question, Phillips posited that in coming years there will be a net outflow of Asian-American scholars and business people to their homelands, boosting the odds that the world's greatest economic power a century from now could be China. "Hegemons of the future are Asian," Phillips said, "and their central banks are the major owners of our debt."

Phillips's remarks immediately prompted a lively discussion among the PIMCO managers. The first wave of comments and questions came from the men and women at the conference table itself—in the main, the firm's managing directors and other key executives. With Gross at the head of the table, McCulley sat at the other end. A few seats to his right was Mohamed El-Erian, chief of PIMCO's emerging markets portfolios, Lee Thomas III, McCulley's corresponding number for global bonds, and William Powers, a senior strategist and mortgage-bond expert. On McCulley's immediate left was Chris Dialynas, another of Gross's inner circle who, as a former student of Nobel Prize-winner Myron Scholes, pioneered options pricing and analysis at PIMCO. A few seats down, opposite Powers, was John Brynjolfsson, whose multisyllabic Icelandic name makes him "Brynjo" to his colleagues. His expertise is in Treasury Inflation-Protected Securities (TIPS) which, though inflation declined steadily in the 1990s, enjoyed a huge rally after their introduction, which was still in full swing as the meeting began. But participation quickly spread to other staff members in the student chairs that flanked the table on both sides, and from the other conference rooms. Phillips himself was grilled for an hour, and then the staff debated the issues he had raised for another hour.

Phillips's gloomy view was reinforced after a lunch break by the bleak analysis of another social critic, William Greider. Greider is author of *One World, Ready or Not: The Manic Logic of Global Capitalism* (Simon & Schuster, 1997). The former Washington Post editor and columnist also wrote *Secrets of the Temple* (Touchstone Books, 1987), a rare inside look at the Federal Reserve, and *Who Will Tell The People: The Betrayal of American Democracy* (Simon & Schuster, 1992), an indictment of the nation's political power brokers published on the eve of Bill Clinton's election. The reading that Greider supplied to participants was an essay titled "Military Globalism," in which he asks, "Can free-market globalization survive in a world governed by one nation's overwhelming military power?" His answer was no—and he cited one of his hosts, Paul McCulley, as sharing his views. In his own "Fed Focus" newsletter, McCulley had written, "American imperialism is, by definition, a retreat away from global capitalism, a retreat from the invisible hand of markets in favor of a more dominant role for the visible fist of governments."

But if Big Government was the target of Greider's essay, his remarks were focused on Big Corporations. They are "the engines of destruction in our society," he asserted. They are "afraid of the future." They are socially irresponsible in fouling the planet with pollutants and fouling society with callous greed. The consequences of their actions over the last 25 years have been rampant consumerism that forces people to work longer hours, to supply more workers per household and to amass an unsustainable level of personal debt. The implications for the future are that American capitalism must reflect different values—concern for families, communities, and the environment—or precipitate social upheaval as progressives and reactionaries fight over the levers of economic power. Greider's comments had particular force because they came amid mounting revelations of shocking corporate greed that destroyed entire companies like Enron and Arthur Andersen, busted WorldCom's shareholders and sent ImClone's founder to prison. Soon the board of the New York Stock Exchange would be shaken apart over the poor judgment it showed in approving extravagant compensation of the then-chief executive. Each scandal handed fresh ammunition to critics like Greider who want to substitute their own hands for Adam Smith's invisible one. Transparency is an issue on which those critics and bond investors readily agree.

One thing investors can take from the conference is the wide-ranging, almost philosophical nature of Bill Gross's interest in and curiosity about the world. The movements of the world's bond markets reflect the consensus of investors' opinions and predictions about every aspect of the world economy. It is almost as if, at any given moment, the key players in the fixed income markets—central banks (like the Fed), institutional investors, governments, and individuals trying to make a buck with their retirement funds—continually assess and project the economic health of the planet. They are constantly taking the world's temperature, trying to spot where things will improve and where prior success is no guarantee of future results.

This consensus expresses itself moment-by-moment on the bond markets' self portrait, the yield curve. The yield curve for Treasuries and the government debt of other stable, prosperous countries is insulated, as we will explore, from all risks except inflation risk. The curve, the expression of the prices investors will pay for debt of different maturities, shows the consensus inflation forecast for each market in which the curve is drawn. Bond prices of corporates across the globe reflect, in a similar way, the average investor's view of inflation risk and credit risk. When one examines the prices of mortgage bonds, other risks, such as prepayment risk, are thrown into the mix—put simply, mortgage bond prices reflect a prediction of the future of real estate markets. And while the domestic currency prices of overseas bonds do not exactly reflect it (the mathematical relationship is complex), forecasts of currency prices are expressed in their movements.

Day Two of the Forum began at 7 A.M. with a presentation by Steve Kandarian, executive director of the Pension Benefit Guaranty Corporation (PBGC), a part of the Department of Labor that insures traditional private pension plans. His agency is virtually unknown to the public, but Kandarian is the most knowledgeable individual in the government on pension matters. Pensions are the United States' biggest block of investment assets—some $3.658 trillion at the end of 2002, just in private plans—and pension policy plays out most vividly in the funding requirements of the kind of huge American companies that provide them. Simply stated, the more monies that corporations plough into pensions, the less they can spend on their business. The level of capital spending is one of the economy's crucial building blocks; it was the utter collapse of spending on telecommunications infrastructure that burst the technology bubble of 1999.

The PBGC was created by the Employee Retirement Income Security Act of 1974 (ERISA). Nearly 44 million Americans are covered by the PBGC's benefits, and ERISA looms very large in the investment world. ERISA sets the standards by which financial fiduciaries—those entrusted with other people's money—are regulated. These are the investment firms, including PIMCO, that invest pension monies under the supervision of sponsoring employers and the Department of Labor. As a firm, PIMCO owes its success greatly to ERISA, which put the government's stamp of approval on the kind of expert, independent money management the firm began offering only a few years before the act was passed by Congress. (The modern-day plans called 401(k) take their name from the paragraph in ERISA that created them.)

Traditional pensions are in decline, Kandarian noted. Since 1986, some 97,000 plans have been terminated; only 32,000 remain. They continue to be offered mainly by old, mature corporations in declining sectors like manufacturing. The guarantee system itself is struggling. It ended its most recent fiscal year with a deficit in its insurance program of $3.6 billion, down from a $7.7 billion surplus only one year earlier. The PBGC sustains itself not on tax dollars but mainly on premiums paid by its dwindling number of members. The financial pressures on them are enormous. Currently, he said, they owe their pension plans $300 billion. These are funds they are required to come up with, even at the expense of investing in their businesses. The ebbing fortunes of the pension industry are yet one more dark cloud hanging over financial markets, Kandarian concluded.

The air of gloom hanging over the PIMCO conference room during the forum, by the way, was not unusual. Fixed-income investments have only one upside: getting your money back. Stock investors harvest dreams; bond investors nurture nightmares. It is in the nature of their "no-upside" world that fixed-income investors see clouds where equity investors see silver linings. The difference between bond and equity investors is profound and, because equities usually command much more public attention, is inevitably cast into sharp relief when the two camps collide. Six weeks after the forum, McCulley delivered remarks to an investment conference in Chicago, echoing many of the concerns the forum had raised, that prompted his co-panelist, Morgan Stanley equity strategist Myron Wien, to remark, "That's the most depressing thing I've ever heard." The equity-heavy audience applauded Wien appreciatively; equity investors prefer good news.

Kandarian was followed by Robert Arnott, editor of the Financial Analysts Journal. He is also a professional investor and chairman of two investment firms: Research Affiliates and First Quadrant. His expertise is in asset allocation, and as a sub-adviser he manages PIMCO All Asset Fund, which invests in a varying mix of other PIMCO funds, including StocksPlus as well as bond funds. Thus he brings to PIMCO, and brought to the forum, the perspective of an investor not solely fixed on bonds. This perspective, nonetheless, was entirely in keeping with the meeting's dolorous mood.

Although he sometimes invests in stocks, at the forum he was singing in the anvil chorus. "We are likely in the early stages of a secular bear market, which will likely span several market cycles," he asserted. This is a controversial view, but one that was very comfortable to the PIMCO team. It translates into a sideways movement of equity prices, rather than the steady climb they enjoy in a secular bull market, of the type the nation experienced from 1982 to 2000. The average secular bear market lasts just as long, Arnott noted—19 years.

A secular bear market puts stocks at a disadvantage to bonds. Historically, stocks have provided after-inflation returns of about 7 percent, which they got from a 4.3 percent dividend rate, a 1.1 percent rate of real earnings growth, and 1.5 percent from the expansion of the multiple to earnings, or premium, they were able to command. But the dividend rate on the Standard & Poor's index has fallen to 1.8 percent and the expansion of the multiple has fallen to zero. Combining dividends and growth implies a future return for stocks of just 2.9 percent, Arnott said—about in line with Treasury Inflation Protected Securities, which are risk-free bonds. Bill Gross has written on this theme for years. When stocks and bonds offer similar returns, bonds are always preferable because their risk is less. At the time Arnott spoke, PIMCO's All Asset Fund held no stocks at all.

If Arnott was preaching to the choir, you would not know it from the questions that rained down on him from all corners of the conference hall. El-Erian ripped into comparisons Arnott had made between the American and Japanese economies. Another questioner said Arnott's fears about declining retirement incomes were overdrawn. Gross himself commented that Arnott's prediction of declining housing prices is not likely to unfold within the time horizon of the secular forum.

The hallmark of the Secular Forum is these exchanges among PIMCO's investment managers. They are what diplomats call "candid." Managers flatly contradicted each other repeatedly, volleying statistics like tennis balls. Assertions were questioned and facts nailed down mercilessly. At one point McCulley and Lee Thomas became so entangled in an argument they begin to shout. Real anger was rare at the meeting, but disagreements were constant. Gross moderated rather than debated, and easily defused flashpoints; when there was a pause between McCulley and Thomas, he laughed, "Paul, I've got two questions for you. No. 1, can I have some of your testosterone?"

The final speaker was Feldstein, who was introduced as "the next Fed chairman." Fed watching is high art at PIMCO, as at any fixed-income investment shop, and future governors are not strangers to this conclave. At the forum in 2000, Princeton University economist Ben Barnanke laid out his views on central banking shortly before he was called to help implement them as a Fed governor.

Feldstein had contributed the fattest collection of readings to the folder, including a paper entitled, "The Role for Discretionary Fiscal Policy in a Low Interest Rate Environment." Fiscal policy is yang to the government's monetary policy yin. Feldstein described opportunities for the federal government to stimulate the economy through highly targeted initiatives such as investment tax credits. But he also had plenty of water to throw on the logs. The nation's savings rate, as high as 8 percent in 1990, has shriveled to 3.6 percent. Pushing it back up shrinks consumer demand, the principal ingredient in global growth. But capital is needed for investment, too, and demographics are pushing the opposite way. Baby boomers are approaching retirement age and retirees are "dis-savers"—they draw on their nest eggs to live. Among those of working age, meanwhile, other impediments to growth clamor for attention. Many jobs have been lost, Feldstein noted, because productivity improvements rendered them redundant. The worst fear of a generation ago—that people would be replaced by machines—has come true in nearly every office, shop, and factory. Among other things, this new employment reality will strip American GDP growth in coming years of one-quarter of its potential, dragging it down to 3 percent annually, he asserted. GDP itself is being diverted from productive to unproductive uses. Entitlement programs are claiming an ever-greater share of domestic output: Social Security and Medicare currently account for 7 percent of GDP, and this will rise to 12 percent by 2030,

Feldstein argued. As if all of this were not enough to worry us, the current account deficit is more likely to rise than to shrink, he added.

One of the few cheerful opinions he contributed is that a so-called bubble in the nation's residential property market was a chimera. Steadily rising housing prices nationwide had fueled concerns that they are unsustainably high. Housing was one of the few sectors of the economy that escaped the recession, and cash put into consumers' hands through mortgage refinancings was a big reason why it was relatively mild. Feldstein argued that the average home price increase to $230,000 from $170,000 was attributable entirely to declining mortgage interest rates, which kept house payments steady even as home prices rose. Indeed, the one enabled the other.

The forum's third and final day was devoted almost entirely to a group discussion of the issues raised in the first two days and how they should impact the firm's investment portfolios. In title the forum is advisory only, with actual decisions left to the firm's investment committee. In reality, all the members of that committee were sitting in the conference hall, and while they shaped the conversation the firm's more-junior portfolio managers, analysts, and account executives contributed most of the questions and comments, often by speakerphone from other conference rooms and from offices in Asia. If such freewheeling discourse with senior management were the norm at American companies, "Dilbert" would not lead the funny papers.

Gross shortly unveiled PIMCO's secular themes in his "Investment Outlook" newsletter. Equity investors will react to them like Myron Wien reacted to Paul McCulley. In the aftermath of the bursting of the stock market bubble in 2000, which destroyed trillions of dollars of wealth, the years to come will find corporations and individuals retiring debt, which will leave demand trailing behind supply. Corporations will fund pensions, build reserves, and deleverage themselves by retiring bonds—they will not spend. The almost never-ending recession in Japan, and a new one in Europe in 2003, throws more water on logs already saturated by the aftereffects of September 11 and SARS. A future terrorist attack would produce instant economic calamity, and wars and fear of wars will cause continuing uncertainty, which destroys business and consumer confidence. Gross's forecast for GDP growth is the same as Feldstein's—just 3 percent.

Gross's other conclusions: China will continue to grab manufacturing share from the developed world, Japan will remain mired in disarray, and the European Union's "Stability Pact" on deficits will inhibit its economies from quick and strong recovery. The current account deficit represents Americans overspending by nearly 6 percent of GDP, another huge drag. The Fed will win its fight against deflation, however, so U.S. interest rates will remain above zero. Gross foresees inflation stabilizing in a band between 2 percent to 3 percent in the United States and 1 percent to 2 percent in Europe. Only Japan will experience no inflation, and possibly will continue to suffer mild deflation.

In this pay-the-piper world, the era of capital gains on Treasury bonds—the salad days—is finished. This is not to say they face a bear market—Gross did not predict the June–July debacle—but they will fly in the face of higher interest rates. By capturing carry and enjoying the hidden benefits of "roll down"—the almost magical increase in price as a Treasury bond becomes one year closer to redemption every 12 months—bond investors can expect real returns from the highest quality of bonds. "The days of eating salad may be over," he wrote after the conference, "but 5 percent is ample sustenance in a low inflationary environment." TIPS will remain attractive.

Gross expects that a rally in corporate bonds, including high-yield, that began one year earlier will peter out. But a handful of other opportunities beckon, notably European government bonds, which offer richer yields than their U.S. counterparts, and municipal bonds, which for a variety of reasons were offering yields in 2003 nearly as high as Treasuries—which means one-third higher after taxes, from which they are exempt.

Gross's critics, and they are legion in the world of stock investing, argue that this outlook constitutes Gross "talking his book"—promoting the very securities he owns. Nearly every professional investor does that; CNBC and Wall Street Week would be bereft of programming if they did not. The exception proves the rule: Fidelity Investments, the nation's largest mutual fund company, has a formal policy prohibiting its managers for commenting on their current buys and sells. As the nation's largest trader of stocks, accounting for between 8 percent and 12 percent of the daily volume on both the New York Stock Exchange and the NASDAQ Stock Market, however, Fidelity would shoot itself in the foot if it telegraphed its trades, pushing up prices of stocks it was buying and destroying those it was selling.

So Fidelity does not talk its book, but in that sense neither does Gross. Bond investors are Joe Btfsplk, the character in the old "Li'l Abner" comic strip who walked around with a perpetual rain cloud over his head; they are always worried about something. For investors in general, however, the most valuable information is the accurate kind. Events will tell how accurately 2003's Secular Forum divined the future: Japanese equities staged a powerful rally in 2003 that began almost the day the forum was held as Japan's economy seemed finally to be gaining traction after years of disappointment. And certainly Gross's crystal ball did not reveal the swift suddenness with which the market's salad days ended: PIMCO Total Return's loss of 3.75 percent in July was the worst one-month decline in its history. Over the fund's existence, however, and before that when PIMCO was purely an institutional investor, the firm has beaten its rivals, and it attributes that success in large measure to its secular thinking. As subsequent chapters will explore, investors who want to learn from Gross will have to adopt a similar long-term outlook. But before I explain ways investors can emulate Gross and develop a "secular forum" of their own, I am going to explain the basics of bond investing. By reading this book, you will develop the ability to build and trade a bond portfolio according to Gross techniques. But first, a primer on the bond market.

CHAPTER 5

All Bonds Are Divided into Three Parts

If you are more familiar with stocks than bonds, be careful: Bond investing is a completely foreign territory, a land governed by different customs and rules. You may be a stranger here, and this world takes some getting used to. You have to change your entire mindset before you can become a serious bond investor. In the next three chapters, I explain the basics of bond investing, and I hope to familiarize you with the language, theory, and laws of the bond market.

An old Wall Street axiom holds that the fundamental difference between bond and stock investors is that stock investors see the sky, and bond investors see the ceiling. If you pick a great stock, and invest in it, you become part owner of a company, and, while there is always the chance that the entire enterprise will go bust, if the company grows, your stake grows along with it. You can buy some penny stocks in a new business, and, if it becomes the next Microsoft, *zap!* You're a millionaire. If you buy bonds, you are engaging in a much simpler transaction. You are simply lending money to companies, expecting to be repaid with interest. You can buy some 5-year bonds paying 9 percent on the day the company opens and five years later, you get your principal back plus that 9 percent coupon.

If you become a serious bond investor, you must remove optimism from investing. "There is no more upside for a bondholder than an issuer not going broke!" says Paul McCulley, the PIMCO partner who shadows the Federal Reserve, divining the meaning of its hints, shrugs, and intentionally obfuscatory ramblings, and the author of a monthly column called "Fed Watch." McCulley, an economist, has been named an all-star bond analyst six times by *Institutional Investor* magazine. He is now one of the 10 most senior members of PIMCO, sitting on the investment committee with the man whose office is next door to his, Bill Gross. He is a Democrat, which is not unique at PIMCO— cofounder Bill Podlich is, too—but is unusual. These people pay their taxes by armored truck. Gross is a Republican and Orange County is as Republican as California gets.

They often say Democrats like to focus on the dark side of life while Republicans focus on the sunny side. If this is true, one would expect the entire bond management field to be populated with hard-core, "yellow dog" Democrats, for bond analysis required the exact opposite of stock analysis: jitters, anxiety, and pessimism.

"Bond's don't pay back 110 percent!" McCulley explains. "Your up-side is defined as getting your money back. On the equity side you have a more symmetrical frame of reference. An equity guy tends to focus on the potential upside. It arouses his animal spirits!" He says this with his bristling eyebrows arching and his smile nearly visible beneath his Yosemite Sam mustache. He says it the way an evangelist speaks of sin—his slight Southern drawl and brimstone message have reminded more than one visitor of a Baptist preacher, which his father is.

The stock market reads Horatio Alger and the bond market reads William Blake. The fearful symmetry of bonds is that they rise when people cry and fall when they laugh. This is why removing the opti-mism is not so bad. In exchange, you also get to remove much of the risk from your investments, and, in bad times, you get a great cushion. It is all because of interest rates. On the bond market's fulcrum, rates and bond prices are always in equilibrium because when one goes down the other goes up in exact proportion. This is simply because, when rates rise, the price of previously issued bonds (paying interest at lower rates than newly issued bonds) drops. In times of great economic hoopla, when rates are rising, stocks usually go up and bonds decline. The time when bonds pay their way is when rates are dropping, the bear is in town, and stock prices are getting more depressed every day. This is when the bond guys and gals are the only people left on Wall Street smiling.

Bonds had three glorious years between 2000 and 2002, when the equity side was melting down. Just as the stock market began to rally in 2003, bonds slipped into red ink. The fact that the two asset classes behave in opposite ways has been obscured for the last 20 years because both enjoyed unprecedented bull markets, which began for bonds in 1981 and for stocks in 1982. This was a coincidence not likely to be repeated in our lifetimes: Both sectors benefited from inflation tumbling to modern-day lows from modern-day highs. Absent such an epochal event, bonds flourish when stocks do not, and vice versa. Most investment advisers urge their clients to have balanced portfolios—some measure of both stocks and bonds—to take advantage of this diversification benefit. Few would advise you put 100 percent of your portfolio into bonds. However, if you are older, need more income, and can bear less risk, you should have the majority of your portfolio in bonds.

Bonds are appealing in their own right, apart from this ability to diversify an equity portfolio—and not only because they provide a predictable stream of income. Gross's total return approach holds out the opportunity for capital appreciation as well as capital preservation. This is one of the most confusing ideas for bond novices to grasp. It would seem as if the smartest way to play bonds would be to buy them, hold them to maturity, and collect the entire coupon (interest payment).

But it is not. While that strategy does not involve much downside risk, it eliminates the considerable upside than can come from bond trading. The smartest and most successful operators in the fixed income market buy and sell bonds constantly, making lots of tiny profits that add up by the end of the year to produce a good return.

Bonds are not a homogeneous group. Like Gaul, they are divided into three parts. The first part involves taxable domestic securities, including Treasuries, mortgages, and corporates. The second part, which is different enough from the first to be treated separately in Chapter Six, is made up of tax-free domestic bonds issued by state and local governments. Together these two groups comprise a $14 trillion marketplace. The third, which again is different enough to merit its own treatment in Chapter Seven, contains foreign bonds. Most investors, and all who favor the Bill Gross approach, will own all three types. Nearly all investors own at least one—the most commonly held by individual investors are domestic taxable bonds (like Treasury bills). These are the most familiar and the most abundant. Even a child's college fund will own bonds like these, at least when the child is approaching matriculation.

Notwithstanding their desire to increase total return, bond investors' first and highest goal is capital preservation. Anything that threatens this has to be taken into account. Bonds are attractive to investors because their risks are so much lower than the risks associated with stocks. You do not get that great upside that can come from buying Apple, Amazon.com, or Intel when those companies are in their infancies. But you also avoid the downside of holding stocks that can lose huge percentages of their market value when bad news hits the wires. The traditional, pre-Gross theory has been that stocks are the place to gamble a bit and hope for an upside; bonds are where you hold your rainy-day money, the money you cannot possibly risk losing, the money that has to provide your income. In the third section of this book, using Gross's Total Return strategy, I take issue with this old saw and recommend you accept more risk in your bond portfolio. However, since bonds are where most investors put funds they want exposed to less risk, the need for capital preservation above all else forces bond investors to be extremely sensitive to all of the risks involved in buying a particular bond issue. In order, the most dangerous risks are: inflation risk, credit risk, and liquidity risk.[1]

Inflation Risk

Fixed-income investors are justifiably obsessed with risk, since their securities have no upside except being serviced and redeemed. This concern can be taken too far, and often is. In the depths of the bear market, legions of ordinary people, whose only exposure to investing was their IRA or 401 (k) plan, became so terrified of losing still more of their money that they cashed out of bonds as well as stocks and went into money markets or bank certificates of deposit. Unwittingly, they were accepting a huge risk that money markets cannot mitigate—the risk of losing purchasing power. A 1 percent return on a money market fund is a negative return when inflation is running close to 2 percent, and an even bigger financial sink hole when tax time comes. Even short-term bonds deliver positive after-inflation and after-tax returns. In the 10 years ended July 31, 2003, McCulley's PIMCO Short-Term Bond Fund returned an annual average of 5.56 percent (versus a rise in the CPI over that period of 25 percent, an equivalent compound rate of 2.24 percent).

In a sense, inflation risk is built into bonds, that is, their yields have to compensate investors for this risk in order for them to find buyers. But they only have to do this the day they are issued. In that sense they are like a new car: The warranty covers manufacturer's

---

[1] Two other important risks, prepayment risk and equity risk, do not apply to all taxable bonds and will be discussed later in the chapter when I discuss mortgage bonds and corporate bonds.

defects but not wear and tear. The moment a bond slips into public hands it is as prone as all the others already out there to be buffeted by changing interest rates. Rates in turn reflect inflation, and the expectation of inflation, so inflation is the No. 1 risk that fixed-income investors face. Unlike the equity hounds who love news of growth in the economy, bond investors welcome any negative news about inflation. Bondholders prefer environments in which the rates of inflation and even growth are decreasing.[2]

As these words are written, inflation is low but the fear of inflation is high. From 1981 to the middle of 2003, the Federal Reserve was single-minded in its efforts to tear inflation root and branch from the U.S. economy. It succeeded—possibly too well. The current core inflation rate is close to zero. In the spring of 2003, the Fed declared this to be ominous, arguing that zero inflation was the platform on the ramp down to deflation. Japan has been deflating intermittently for more than a decade, and its economy has gone from being the most vibrant in the world to the least, at least among developed nations. Deflation was what made the Depression "Great," and as surely as rampant inflation fueled the fires of fascism in 1920s Germany, deflation did the same for communism in 1930s America. McCulley has called it "the burden the beast of Capitalism cannot bear": Capitalism comes apart at the seams when prices fall relentlessly, as the economic system, unlike a computer, has no mechanism that allows it to reboot.

The prevailing theory among economists since Keynes has been that only government spending can reverse such declines; hence Roosevelt's New Deal and the importance of "priming the pump." Thus in June 2003, the Fed's Open Market Committee made its remarkable announcement, declaring the war against inflation to be won, and the

---

[2]This is *not* to say that bond investors prefer negative rates of growth or deflation, which can have very bad effects on the bond market; they prefer an environment in which the rates, while positive, are flat or decreasing from month to month.

one against its opposite to be begun. "The probability, though minor, of an unwelcome substantial fall in inflation exceeds that of a pickup in inflation from its already low level," it said, and added that this concern would dominate policy "for the foreseeable future." The central bank cut already-low short-term interest rates, while at the same time inflation-panicked investors dumped so many 10-year Treasury notes that their yield surged 40 percent in six weeks.

This example shows how expectations of inflation, more than actual changes in the rate, influence the prices of bonds. This is made more complex by the fact that the bond market constantly prices in investors' expectations of what inflation may be at many different time periods. Treasuries are issued by the U.S. government at a variety of different maturity dates; the price of the 1-year, 5-year, and 10-year bonds fluctuates as investors estimate what inflation may be one, five, and ten years from now.

If interest rates are plotted on a graph and the dots are connected, they typically describe an upward sloping curve, an arch that rises sharply at first and then smoothes itself almost straight. This is called the *yield curve*, and is the basis for analysis of how the yield offered on new bonds is affected by their maturity. The normal yield curve displays greater distance between short and intermediate rates than between intermediate and long; the slope levels off as it extends. After the Fed acted in June 2003, short rates were 1 percent, the 10-year a little over 4 percent, and the 30-year just over 5 percent. Before it acted, the curve had been distorted—more a straight 45-degree line than a curve, the rates being 1.25 percent, 3.1 percent and 5 percent, respectively. Seeing this, Gross declared that Treasury bonds (this is, the Treasury yield curve) were in a bubble; relatively high prices for the intermediate maturity Treasury, the 10-year note, had pushed its yield too far down. A dose of inflation fear shocked it into something closer to normal. A steep curve such as this usually means the market thinks the bull's in town: great news for equity investors, but a "sell" signal for bondholders.

On rare occasions the yield curve will become a sloping, inverted curve. This happens when interest rates paid on long-maturity bonds are lower than the rates for short-term bonds, as when 5-year Treasuries or 1-year Treasuries pay more annually than 10-year bonds. This paradoxical situation occurs when pessimistic bond investors take the plunge into out-and-out gloom. They come to believe that rates have so far to fall that, in the future, they are going to be less high than they will be in the next year or so. Some commentators believed the curve might invert after September 11, 2001 on the theory that short-term spending to recover from the disaster would push the economy and rates up, only to have the party fizzle out, sending rates back down a few years later. The curve inverted in 2000 at the height of the boom, when investors realized things were going to get tough, and rates had the potential to drop substantially over several years (as indeed they did); the curve also inverted in 1980 before the plunge that preceded the Reagan tax cuts.

The inverted yield curve is seen as a sure sign that the market is predicting a recession. In order for the curve to go from normal to inverted, it passes through an intermediate stage where it appears to be flat or "humped" (a humped curve is one in which medium-term bonds have higher rates than either short-term or long-term). This is seen by many as an early recession predictor, a theory born out in 1990 when a humped curve anticipated the post-Gulf War recession.

These different curve forms illustrate how closely bond yields are linked to investors' expectations of inflation. Stock addicts regularly "read" the government bond yield curves to see, written out before their eyes, the consensus view on what is going to happen in the economy, and hence the market. (See Figure 5.1.)

To assess the potential risks involved in buying a bond, investors do not just look at their expectations for future inflation: They also calculate the bond's duration. This calculation shows investors how much interest rate risk is involved in buying the bond. It answers the question: Just how sensitive will this bond's price be to increases and decreases in the rates? This calculation is complex but essential.

Figure 5.1   U.S. Yield Curve, 2003

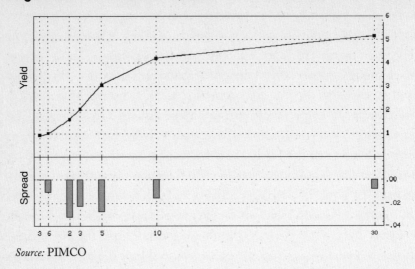

Source: PIMCO

The mathematical explanation is this: Duration is the mathematical calculation of a bond's sensitivity to changes in interest rates—the change in the price of the bond divided by the change in interest rates equals duration. Conceptually, duration is maturity adjusted for early return of capital, a calculation that produces a figure similar to the discounted present value of the bond.

When part of a long bond's total returns are paid upfront, in the form of current interest, the bond's duration shortens, and it becomes less sensitive to rate changes because it has paid out part of its coupon. Two-thirds of the entire income potential of a 30-year bond will have been exhausted in the first 20 years; as these payments are made, the duration of the long bond falls. Calls on corporates and prepayments on mortgages can also reduce their duration sharply. There is an exception to this rule, however—zero-coupon bonds. These are securities that pay no current interest until their maturation; Wall Street has stripped the coupons and sold them to other investors. Since they pay no interest at all until they mature, these bonds' duration is exactly the same as their maturity. This is easiest to understand when you consider a 30-year zero-coupon Treasury bond. It cannot be called; maturity is the same as duration, because you will not receive the economic benefit, even in part, for 30 years. As a result, it has maximum sensitivity to changing interest rates. Think of it this way: The zero-coupon bond will give investors a fixed rate of return on their money. Every day, as interest rates change, that return will look better or worse: more or less attractive to investors (with interest rates in an inverse relationship to the return rate of the bond). A conventional Treasury, however, pays interest twice a year; you receive immediate and continuing economic benefit. In the same way, a Treasury's value is constantly recalculated in the market (via movements in price) as rates go up or down, making its coupon more or less attractive. But because the coupon on a long bond that has been around a while has been partially paid out, it is less sensitive to risk than a zero-coupon on which nothing has been paid out. The Treasury's duration is less than maturity because a change in rates affects only part of the total value of the bond; the impact on the revenue stream is less than on the principal. Since much of its interest has been paid out, the only calculation investors need to make is whether the diminished fractional payment to come still seems attractive compared to current rates. Measuring duration is difficult: The exact calculation is complex. You need a thorough analysis of the bond's characteristics and a computer. Fortunately, to determine the duration of a bond, investors needs only look on Bloomberg or subscribe to a bond pricing service.

PIMCO Total Return manages duration along two lines, depending on the shape of the yield curve. Both are intended to achieve a blended, or average, duration of between three and six years (this period is considered the best duration through which to seek maximum risk-adjusted return). The first approach, called a bullet, is utilized when the greatest value on the curve is focused on a single point, its intermediate maturities. The second tack, the barbell design, invests at both the long and short end to achieve an average maturity in the intermediate range. As discussed in the section on Treasury bonds, PIMCO Total Return currently is implementing a bullet approach. In the final chapter of this book, I explain how investors can take advantage of these strategies to increase their returns from bonds.

PIMCO does not offer any investment vehicles for individuals to participate in the zero-coupon market, and that is just as well, because they have only two possible uses. One would be to pre-fund an obligation that will fall due in the future. At the end of July, 2003, you could buy a zero-coupon Treasury maturing in 2020 with a face value of $1,000 for about $431. Unfortunately, even though you do not collect semiannual interest on the bond, you must pay income taxes on the imputed amount as though you did, so your economic gain is not quite $569, which works out to be a rate on the bond of 5.0746 percent. Thus, zero-coupons are suitable for tax-insulated accounts like IRAs and not for your ordinary portfolio. Still, for planning purposes zeros can be efficient—assuming you absolutely will not sell it before maturity. But these bonds are very illiquid (hard to trade) and they are so sensitive to interest rate fluctuations that investing in them for the short term is extremely risky. Save them for your biggest Grossian bets.

The other useful role these bonds fill is satisfying the needs of interest-rate speculators. These are the longest-duration bonds there are, and immune to any risk but fluctuations in interest rates, so their sensitivity to such fluctuations is extreme. In the case of 2020 zeros, prices shot up about 22 percent in 2002, as rates were falling. Their even longer siblings, 2030s, surged more than 29 percent. When they fall, it is usually in double digits, too. This is the most extreme volatility the fixed-income world experiences, and so distant from capital preservation as to be like a polar bear in the swimming pool. Making informed bets about the direction of interest rates is one thing; speculating at the risk of 30 percent losses is another, inadvisable for all but the world's least nervous gamblers.

Credit Risk

The next level of bond risk after interest rate risk is credit risk. This is the risk that a company will default on its bond obligations. Although bondholders hold a more privileged status than common and preferred stockholders in the event of a bankruptcy, they still risk losing their money if the bond-issuing company goes completely belly-up. Corporate bonds are rated according to the creditworthiness of their issuers (see Table 5.1). The main rating agencies are Moody's Investors Service and Standard & Poor's Corp. Their nomenclature is slightly different. Moody's rating is Aaa while for S&P it is AAA. Other investment-grade rankings—the only type suitable for most institutions, like bank trust departments—are double and single A and triple B. High yield, or junk, bonds are rated from B to C. If you do not earn at least a C in this market, you are expelled because your bonds are worthless.

Table 5.1   Common Rating Terminology

Moody's	S&P	Definition
Investment Grade		
Aaa	AAA	Best quality
Aa	AA	Next best quality
A	A	Upper-medium grade
Baa	BBB	Medium grade
High-Yield or Junk		
Ba	BB	Speculative; major ongoing uncertainties
B	B	Repayment assurance in doubt
Caa	CCC	Poor; may be in default
Ca	CC	Often in default
C	C	Repayment assurance almost nil
Note: Moody's ratings may have numerals after the letters, from 1 to 3, indicating degrees of quality within the category: A1 is superior to A2, which is superior to A3. *Sources*: Moody's Investors Service; Standard & Poor's Corp.		

Even the finest corporation with the soundest balance sheet and safe-as-houses bonds can run into trouble. Amid the financial tumult of the 1990s, the bonds of nearly all telecommunications companies, including the venerable Lucent Technologies, parent of Bell Laboratories and child of Ma Bell herself, fell into the junk bin (grades of Ba/BB or lower are referred to as "junk," or, since the 1980s made the term infamous, "high-yield bonds"). Downgrades of top-rated debt are not uncommon. In addition to rating new bonds, the agencies monitor existing issues, and upgrade and downgrade them depending on the financial health of their issuer.

Liquidity Risk

Another risk of bonds is the chance their owners will not be able to sell them when they need to: This is liquidity risk. Just as very thinly traded stocks can be hard to sell, if you find yourself holding very obscure or unusual bond issues, you will have to pay unusually high commissions if you want to sell them (bond commissions are usually hidden in the quoted price—so they are hard to spot, unless they are unusually high). Additionally, just as with stocks, there is not much information available on unusual, obscure bonds, and they can be correspondingly difficult to research and monitor. However—remember the Efficient Markets Theory—these obscure bonds are sometimes slow to react to news; rather than shun them, many experts stock up on them, hoping to take advantage of mispricings to capitalize on the inefficiencies of this market. But while obscure bonds offer some routes to profit, professionals treat illiquid bonds gingerly. Gross's own Orange County went bankrupt in the 1990s when it got caught with too many illiquid bonds in its portfolio. The most spectacular liquidity crisis of recent years was the events leading up to the collapse of Long Term Capital Management (LTCM), a hedge fund than ran aground on shoals of risk that the firm's principals, notably Myron Scholes, did not foresee.

LTCM invested in fixed-income securities around the world, using Black-Scholes options theory to take advantage of tiny disparities between securities prices that its computers predicted would disappear. Scholes won the Nobel Prize for his work—and Fisher Black would have had he not died. Scholes shared the prize with Robert Merton, another LTCM principal, who in essence argued that the firm could eliminate all risk. John Meriwether, who had established a sterling (albeit controversial) record as a Salomon Brothers bond trader, rounded out what one news account termed "the team of the century." The fund delivered returns to its investors of 20 percent in its first year (1994), 43 percent in the second and 41 percent in the third.

The hedge fund was tripped up by liquidity risk. First, its basic strategy began to misfire. In one instance of many, it had loaded up on 29-year Treasuries because they were yielding 5 basis points more than their 30-year twins. This defied logic, so the firm shorted the 30s to neutralize the trade, and waited for the 5 points to disappear. They did not; they increased to 15, a very surprising result. Much more ominously, in 1997 the Asian Crisis devastated emerging markets, and 1998's default by Russia on its sovereign debt likewise had never been considered by Black and Scholes. All of a sudden, virtually all the emerging market bonds that LTCM owned became extremely illiquid. No one wanted to buy them. To turn the difficult into the impossible, the hedge fund had leveraged its portfolio an astonishing 240 times, as calculated by *Forbes* magazine; when it began to get margin calls, it could not begin to cover them. It could not sell any of its illiquid debt to pay off the losses generated by the bad call on 29-year Treasuries, among other mistakes. By the fall of 1998, the U.S. Treasury and the Federal Reserve had stepped in to clean up the mess, at a cost to taxpayers of $3.6 billion.

In a fixed-income portfolio, as opposed to a quixotic and highly leveraged hedge fund, bond risks are managed when the investor diversifies throughout the available range of credit instruments available. Experts buy a basket of bonds with different interest rate, credit, and liquidity risks, hoping the low correlation of risks will reduce the volatility of the portfolio. However, a balancing act is always required: The classes of bonds that are perceived to be vulnerable to higher risk have to pay more to attract investors. Sometimes this takes the form of higher yield (junk bonds always have much higher yield than top-rated ones) and, if the bonds are sold by someone other than issuer, this takes the form of lower prices. Naturally, the premium on a very risky bond is lower than that on a very safe one. This is where bargains lie: The riskier the bond, the higher the carry.

This technique demands investors stock their portfolios with different types of bonds. In the world of taxable bonds, the principal choices are these:

Treasuries and Agencies

"Treasuries" are the obligations of the United States government, backed by its full faith and credit, and therefore assumed by investors worldwide to be free from credit risk. They come in bills (which have maturities of one year or less); notes (which have maturities of up to 10 years); and bonds (which are the longest). Thanks to decades of budget deficits as well as the government's own funding requirements, Treasuries are abundant. "Agencies" are the debt of governmental organizations, such as the Government National Mortgage Association. Agency Bonds issued by the mortgage security companies Ginnie Mae and Fannie Mae are distinguished from mortgage pass-throughs because they are the direct debt of the agency itself, not a collection of homeowners' notes.

James Keller, the PIMCO managing director responsible for the firm's government-bond desk, says the anxiety that is native to bond investing is even worse in today's Treasury market. "A very powerful policy-making body, the Federal Reserve, is taking dead aim at your product," he says. "Treasuries tend to do very poorly in an environment when inflation is rising." This is because Treasuries, being highly liquid and lacking any risk of default, are sensitive only to interest rate risk.

Since Treasuries are free of all but interest rate risk, they are managed purely on the basis of duration, seeking to find the optimal point on the yield curve. During the summer of 2003, Keller told me, "We think the middle of the curve, the intermediate maturities, will outperform the long bond because of the combination of coupon and capital gains. For a period such as now, we're focusing primarily on carry per unit of duration, and that means avoiding very long Treasury maturities." This is the bullet, rather than the barbell discussed earlier.

Keller's remarks reflect PIMCO's management of Treasuries in the Total Return fund and similar institutional accounts. The fund he manages, PIMCO Long-Term U.S. Government Fund, which has a duration of 10.5 years, is required by its mandate to stick to the long end of the maturity scale. For buy-and-hold investors this can be an attractive fund. Its annualized 10-year returns of 8.24 percent beat Gross's 7.49 percent. By the same token, those returns reflect a period of falling interest rates, which benefits the long end of the curve the most. The decade to come is more likely to see higher rates, which wreak the most havoc on long bonds.

Inflation-Linked Treasuries

In 1997, investors were delighted when the Treasury Department unveiled Treasury Inflation-Protected Securities, or TIPS. These bonds pay a guaranteed return plus a premium based on increases in the consumer price index (CPI). TIPS are issued in maturities from one to 30 years; the guaranteed coupon goes up with maturity, from 1.0 percent at the short end to 2.8 percent at the long. The idea of TIPS was not an American innovation: Canada, Great Britain, Israel, New Zealand, and Turkey issued inflation-linked government bonds earlier.

"Another name for these is real return bonds, and that's really a more meaningful description of them," says John Brynjolfsson, manager of PIMCO Real Return Fund, which specializes in them. "What they do is allow someone planning for the future to lock in five to 30 years ahead of time not only their current purchasing power but a substantial growth in purchasing power."

Bill Gross regards TIPS as one of the most exciting opportunities for bond investors, professionals and individuals alike, in today's market. In addition to their other attributes, TIPS are relatively scarce, accounting for only about 5 percent of all Treasuries in circulation. This creates a liquidity risk, but, as the bonds yield more than they otherwise would, in response, it also makes them more attractive to investors. This premium is about a quarter of a percentage point. In addition, the tax structure of TIPS makes them harder for individual investors to hold outside tax-deferred structures like IRAs (payments are delayed but TIPS-holders receive an annual tax bill for the imputed income that is costly and unfortunate for individuals holding them in taxable accounts).[3] Yet, as I argue, this tax problem is manageable. TIPS are discussed in more detail in Chapter Eight.

Mortgage Pass-Throughs

The government created this type of bond to provide liquidity to the home-finance market, with the goal of bringing down mortgage interest rates; the plan has succeeded beyond anyone's wildest dreams. Mortgage bonds are now the single biggest segment of the domestic bond market, accounting for more than $8 trillion of debt. Today when

---

[3]TIPS pay out their regular return in the same way as Treasuries, but the "extra" return portion is deferred until maturity. Unfortunately, the IRS calculates the extra return portion each year, and assesses it as part of your tax bill. Thus, with a TIP currently paying out 3 percent plus CPI, you will have to pay income tax each year on an amount likely to be more like 4 percent or 5 percent, depending on inflation, and if inflation rises dramatically, your payments could be rather high. As a result, investors often restrict TIPS to tax-deferred accounts.

a lender grants you a mortgage or refinances an existing one, the note usually ends up somewhere in this vast pool, rather than the vault of the original lender. Each mortgage bond reflects a small slice of this pool, and therefore the payments made on many different individual mortgage loans as well. (Indeed, mortgage lenders typically get their revenue from fees associated with the loan, rather than its interest, which is passed along.)

Mortgage bonds have one characteristic that sets them apart from all others, although it is analogous to the call option on corporate bonds. This is prepayment risk. Generations ago, when people stayed in one place and savings and loan associations relied on mortgages they indeed kept in their vaults for their revenue, homeowners were unable to prepay their note without penalty. That restriction has long since disappeared, and home refinancings were a crucial source of household capital during the recession of 2001 and its aftermath. Scott Simon, who as manager of two PIMCO funds, GNMA and Total Return Mortgage, is particularly close to the subject, refinanced his mortgage six times during this boom, each time bringing down the rate. (This less-agile author managed to do it once.)

Mortgage bonds, therefore, have indeterminate durations. Their durations are calculated, for trading and record keeping purposes, via a formula based on prevailing rates of refinancing, but their durations can change, and usually in a way the bondholder least desires. If rates are falling, refinancings rise and old, higher-yielding mortgages are retired. The bond investor gets his principal back when he least wants it, because new mortgages are yielding less than the old. If rates are rising, the opposite occurs; refinancings slow and the ratio of older, lower-yielding notes within the bond increases, decreasing the bond's overall yield. The duration of the mortgage component of the Lehman Aggregate Bond Index soared to three years, from one, in just six weeks in the summer of 2003—on a one-point rise in mortgage rates. Owing to this risk, mortgages have a lot of carry, up to 2 percentage points over Treasuries, even though their risk is negligible. And for this reason PIMCO has a secular bias in favor of mortgages.

All of these bonds are pure income vehicles without exposure to equity risk. But three important categories of bonds do have such risk, albeit in varying degrees.

High-Quality Corporate Bonds

These are the bread-and-butter tools of corporate financing. They are how General Motors finances itself—as well as General Motors Acceptance Corporation (its credit arm), the carmaker's subsidiaries, and the rest of the Fortune 500.

The most "blue-chip" corporate bonds are those that receive Triple-A ratings, considered by rating agencies to be in no danger that either their principal or interest payments are in the slightest doubt. Doubt increases as credit quality declines, and any investment-grade bond in danger of falling into junk status will almost certainly be sold by a high-quality bond fund before that happens. There are four baskets of credit quality in this universe: AAA, AA, A, and BBB. The lowest investment-grade rating is Triple-B. It is the Triple-B paper that is most vulnerable to the slide into junk status, but this is also the highest-yielding segment of the high-quality group. As mentioned earlier, Gross's Total Return fund (as of its latest portfolio report) had 77 percent of assets in bonds rated Triple-A or backed by the federal government, and 10 percent in Triple-Bs.

The higher a bond's rating, the less credit risk it has. Movements in the issuing corporation's stock price have little effect on high-rated bonds; the most equity-sensitive high-quality bonds, therefore, are those with low ratings like Triple-Bs. If the issuer's stock price takes a beating, investors will flee their bonds fearing default. In the early summer of 2003, Mark Kiesel, co-head of PIMCO's investment-grade corporate desk, stated, "Now is a good time to be buying Triple-B assets." With the economy in recovery, the ability of their issuers to service their bonds is strengthening, but their yields remain relatively higher than this new reality would imply. Also, yields on the highest-quality corporates are relatively low. The result: "The Fed is so stimulative they're forcing you and I to take risk," says Kiesel, who is also co-manager of PIMCO Investment Grade Corporate Fund.

Generally speaking, corporates offer a lot of carry—more than is justified, in Gross's opinion, and therefore they are a favorite of his from time to time. Yields of Triple-A bonds usually are 0.5 percentage points more than Treasuries of comparable maturity. The spread to Triple-B is 1.0 points.

Convertible Securities

These can be stocks or bonds; convertible bonds are senior to the former in a company's capital structure, making them safer and therefore decreasing their yields relative to convertible stock. Following Ed Thorpe's advice, Bill Gross cut his teeth on converts because they are difficult to analyze and therefore offer an informed investor advantages over the market in general.

The classic convert is a bond in all respects except one, which is the convertibility feature. It pays interest semiannually, at a rate established when it is issued, and trades in the secondary market at a price that adjusts the coupon to yields prevailing at the time—more than par if rates have declined, less if they have risen. They are issued in varying maturities. The average duration of the PIMCO Convertibles Fund at the time of writing is 2.0 years.

The convertibility feature is an option (to exchange the bond for stock in the issuing company at a set rate) that has economic value itself, and therefore convertibles tend to yield less than corresponding conventional bonds. The convert option usually can be exercised some years after the bond is issued, at a price significantly higher than the current market value of the company's stock. For example, a bond that trades at 50 might be convertible into 2.5 shares of common stock six years from now, meaning the shares would have to be worth $20 at the time for the option to be in the money. Today's stock price might be

$11. If your analysis of the company's prospects are sufficiently bright to justify a near doubling of its stock price in this period, this option is valuable to you, plus you earn the coupon while you wait.

Some high-quality companies issue converts, but they are utilized more by firms whose self-confidence is stronger than their balance sheet. Their credit ratings are lower—a plurality of bonds in the portfolio of PIMCO Convertibles Fund are rated Single-A, and 77 percent (again) are rated Double-A to Triple-B—so the convertible feature is added to cap their coupon expense.

Taking a view of convertibles assumes you are interested in owning the underlying equity. Gross takes a very dim view of equity at today's prices, and says he owns not a single equity—nada, zip, bupkis. PIMCO Total Return, therefore, has a secular bias against converts.

Below-Investment-Grade Bonds

I told earlier the story of Chris Dialynas persuading Gross to reject the junk bonds being peddled by the then-young Michael Milken of Drexel Burnham Lambert. As their nickname suggests, below-investment-grade bonds are viewed by most bond managers with considerable skepticism, if not outright disdain. If converts are vulnerable to equity risk, junk is even more imperiled. They are issued in the first place by companies whose financial strength is insufficient to persuade rating agencies that they can have confidence the issuers will be able to service the bonds throughout their lives. Such companies may have significant operational difficulties, such as failing products or aging facilities. The group has five baskets, rather than the four of high-quality bonds—BB, B, CCC, CC, and C—and already by grade Single-B the agencies have doubts issuers can meet their coupons, let alone return capital. All three of the C categories reflect bonds that are teetering (to one degree or another) closely to default.

This much risk requires such bonds to pay correspondingly high yields, and indeed the industry delicately refers to them as high-yield bonds; "junk" does not sound very professional. PIMCO High-Yield Fund operates in this marketplace, and as of July 31, 2003, its 12-month yield as reported to the Securities & Exchange Commission was 7.94 percent.

As these words are written, PIMCO is ambivalent about junk bonds. They are the most equity-like of all bonds, because the conditions that create a favorable market for stocks buoy the companies that issue junk and make it easier for them to pay interest and principal. In the 12 months ended July 31, PIMCO High-Yield delivered total returns of 24.61 percent for the same reason that the stock market rallied: The economy was growing noticeably stronger, and the pace of economic growth was accelerating. Another huge plus for the group is that "high-yield assets do well in an inflationary environment," says Raymond Kennedy, manager of the High-Yield fund and a PIMCO partner who sits on Gross's investment committee. Inflation generates higher cash flows for the issuers of such bonds; in a sense, he says, "they reflate away their debt."

That being said, Gross notes that yields on junk have fallen to 8 percent from more than 10 percent, meaning that these values are already reflected in the prices of junk bonds. "High-yield has peaked, at least for this cycle," Kennedy says. In his Total Return portfolio, Gross is extremely sensitive to relative values, and he finds these lacking in junk today. Gross's fund is holding almost no junk.

Constructing a Bond Portfolio

Bond investors have numerous options available to them to construct a fixed-income portfolio. If you just want to dabble and you are not trying to be Bill Gross, the easiest thing to buy is a balanced mutual fund. Balanced funds typically have 60 percent of their assets in equities and 40 percent in cash and bonds. Gross currently takes a dim view of equities, and does not own any himself, so a balanced fund defies his advice. That said, Gross himself manages PIMCO StocksPlus Fund, which uses futures options to mimic the stock market and active bond management to increase total returns. StocksPlus in turn can be, but currently is not, owned by PIMCO All Asset Fund, managed by Robert Arnott, so an all-Gross portfolio can be constructed with equity exposure.

The traditional means by which individuals invest in bonds is the direct purchase of individual securities. This is particularly easy with Treasury securities, including TIPS, which can be purchased directly from the government without commissions. These are electronic-entry certificates that cannot be traded, however. More typically, therefore, total return investors who choose individual securities will work through a brokerage firm or a financial adviser, buying and selling in the secondary market. All brokerage firms are not alike. I would not open a bond-trading account with a firm or (especially) an adviser until I was satisfied they could provide timely research and economical order execution. Bond commissions are buried in the price, unlike stock commissions, which are explicit. If I were to work directly with a discount broker—and some of them are reputed to have excellent bond shops—I would query several for a specific price quote on a bond in which I were interested.

Diversifying a portfolio of individual bonds, and trading them, is not economical for a small account, however; one-way bond trades on a single bond or two can involve an implicit commission on the order of magnitude of 4 percent. Bill Gross recommends a minimum fixed-income portfolio of $500,000 to achieve the necessary diversity and economy of scale. Also, researching individual bonds is considerably more difficult than researching stocks, both because the former are more numerous and because the latter are more popular with the advertisers who support freely available financial publications. While the bear market in stocks has made bonds fashionable because they have been more rewarding than stocks, the "secular bias" of financial editors remains fixed in the firmament. Researching bonds will cost you more than researching stocks, because advertiser-supported media will ignore them as much as possible.

Faced with these obstacles, many bond investors find themselves guided toward professionally managed accounts. Some investment firms offer so-called institutional managed accounts with minimums as low as $100,000. The implication is that management fees will be less than those of public funds, or that they will be only modestly higher while allowing you to tailor your portfolio to your precise needs. Because bond commissions are hidden in the price, it is difficult to evaluate this insinuation. I would be skeptical unless the broker handling the account could satisfactorily explain exactly what the total annual account fees were, including commissions.

Public portfolios divide themselves into conventional mutual funds and closed-end funds. The former are open-end portfolios that allow you to invest at net asset value and redeem your shares, also at net asset value, freely. PIMCO Total Return is such a fund. The advantages of funds are professional management—active management in this case, although bond index funds are available from some fund complexes (but not PIMCO)—as well as thorough portfolio diversification. Mutual funds are convenient and easy to follow; fund-analysis firms like Morningstar and Lipper track bond funds with as much zeal as equity funds, and their data are abundant in newspapers, magazines, online, and at the public library.

Closed-end funds—do not call them "closed-end mutual funds" because they are not mutual in that sense—are significantly different creatures. These are actively managed portfolios of fixed size that are bought and sold like stocks; most are listed on the New York Stock Exchange. Their price is established in the marketplace, and while it will have some relation to net asset value, premiums and (especially) discounts are chronic. Bill Gross uses closed-end funds in his personal portfolio, and one reason is you can often buy a dollar's worth of value for 95 cents and then, when conditions are right, sell it for a buck and a nickel.

Closed-end bond funds tends to be leveraged. Managers issue preferred stock in the fund to institutions and use the spread over their financing costs of the preferred to buy more bonds, thus increasing the portfolio's overall yield. Leverage can work against a portfolio as well as in its favor—when bond prices are falling, the effect is magnified in a leveraged closed-end fund.

Aside from municipal bond funds, which are discussed in the next chapter, PIMCO sponsors five closed-ends, investing in junk bonds, high-quality corporates, mortgages, and global government bonds. Here are snapshot reports on each of them. Data, which are derived from various sources, including *ETFConnect.com*, are as of July 31, 2003, for net asset values, share price, premium/discount, yield on share price, annualized total returns, and premium/discount history; most recent reporting period for net assets; June 30, 2003, for credit quality and duration; and most recent month for dividends.

PIMCO Commercial Mortgage Trust (Ticker Symbol: PCM) Managed by Bill Powers, this fund has assets of $142.1 million and is not leveraged. It has an average credit quality of Single-A and a duration of 4.41 years. The net asset value is $12.23 and the market price $13.95, giving a premium to NAV of 14.06 percent. The current yield on the share price is 8.07 percent. The fund pays a dividend of 9.38 cents monthly. It has delivered annualized returns on its share price of 3.73 percent for one year, 15.54 percent for three years and 10.54 percent for five years. It has consistently traded at a premium to NAV since its inception in 1993.

PIMCO Corporate Income Fund (PCN) Managed by David Hinman, the fund, which is leveraged, has assets of $823.7 million, of which $300 million is preferred shares. The duration is 4.33 years. The net asset value is $14.57 and the share price $14.36, for a discount of 1.44 percent. The current yield on the share price is 8.88 percent. The fund pays a monthly dividend of 10.63 cents. It has delivered annualized returns on its share price of 16.67 percent for the most recent year. Since its inception in 2001, it traded at a premium to NAV until the summer of 2003.

PIMCO High Income Fund (PHK)   Managed by Charles Wyman, this fund was launched in April of 2003, and very little information about it has been developed. It pays a monthly dividend of 12.19 cents. The net asset value is $13.88 and the market price $13.83, giving a discount of 0.36 percent. The current yield on the share price is 10.58 percent.

PIMCO Corporate Opportunity Fund (PTY)   Also managed by David Hinman, this leveraged fund has assets of $1.62 billion, of which $565 million are preferred shares. Its average credit quality is Triple-B and the average duration 5.16 years. The net asset value is $15.92 and the share price $15.31, giving a discount of 3.83 percent. The yield on the share price as of August 19, 2003, was 6.42 percent. The fund pays a monthly dividend of 13.75 cents. It was launched in December 2002, initially trading at a premium to NAV but falling to a discount.

PIMCO Strategic Global Government Fund (RCS)   Managed by Pasi Hamalainen, this unleveraged fund has assets of $395.3 million. Average credit quality is Triple-A. The net asset value is $10.95 and the share price $12.18, giving a premium of 11.23 percent. The yield on the share price as of Aug. 14, 2003, was 7.53 percent. The fund pays a monthly dividend of 7.4 cents. It has delivered average annual returns on its share price of 10.91 percent for one year, 20.87 percent for three years, and 13.91 percent for five years. It has traded at a premium to NAV since its inception in 1994.

As this book was going to press, a new exchange-traded fund was introduced by Barclays Global Investors called iShares Lehman Aggregate Bond Fund. Carrying the ticker symbol AGG, the fund is designed to track the index with an annual expense ratio of 0.2 percent or 20 basic points. Although Vanguard Group is better known to most investors as indexing specialists, Barclays is actually larger. Assuming this fund succeeds in tracking its benchmark reliably, it could be employed as a core portion of a Gross style total-return bond portfolio.

High-quality domestic bonds are facing an uncertain future. With the Fed declaring war on deflation, and thus promising at least moderate inflation, the 20-plus year bull market in bonds is over, and a bear market has begun. With a rising or stable yield curve predicted for the immediate future, double-digit bond returns are history. In a bull market it is literally possible to select successful investments by throwing darts at tables in the *Wall Street Journal*; the paper itself used to publish a regular column illustrating the point, which it discontinued during the bear market for stocks. In a bear market, willy-nilly investing is not possible. Securities selection becomes dominant. In the case of Gross, this means identifying bond sectors that will perform better than others. He makes his fearless forecast in the penultimate chapter of this book. If you have read to this point, you can already appreciate some of these recommendations. The next chapters, on nontaxable bonds and foreign bonds, will add still more to your informational larder.

CHAPTER 6

Taking Taxes
Off the Table

Tax-free investing does not refer to tax-avoidance schemes of the sort that hedge funds, for example, have been known to cook up—the collapse of the Long Term Capital Management Fund ultimately led to lawsuits over such alleged schemes. Nor does it refer to the sort of loopy (and often illegal) tax haven schemes in the Cayman Islands advertised in the back of financial magazines. It does not refer to tax-deferred programs, like pensions and annuities, which have tax characteristics that usually make them inappropriate for municipal bonds (munis) and muni-bond funds. It simply refers to using tax-free municipal bonds as part of your investing portfolio.

If you are a serious investor in a high tax bracket, you will benefit from having both taxable and tax-deferred portfolios. The latter are the better platform for Treasuries and most income-oriented investments, and the former for municipals and growth equities. The ideal nest egg contains both kinds, in as much abundance as you are able to husband.

135

What has become the United States of America was a nation more in name than fact when it was forged from the conflict with Great Britain in 1776. Delegates to the Continental Congress represented states and their cities and farms. The Civil War had to be fought to establish federal primacy over the states. In that war, states and their localities funded much of the cost of fighting, and virtually all of the other expenses of government, notably the construction and maintenance of roads, turnpikes, canals, sanitation and public-water facilities, and the myriad other requirements of an emerging industrial society. Until the twentieth century, equities played a relatively minor role in the formation of capital; as recently as 1926, bonds represented 75 percent of all new securities underwritings.[1] Americans were famously conservative investors: Andrew Carnegie limited his portfolio almost entirely to bonds, not least because in his day stocks were still unregulated and the bond market already had a powerful group of what Bill Gross calls vigilantes who punished borrowers who reneged on their debt. Throughout the nineteenth century, American states and cities routinely tapped global securities markets to meet their financial obligations: The Commonwealth of Pennsylvania announced a $3 million issue at the start of the Civil War to defend itself against the kind of attack that actually occurred in 1863 in Gettysburg. As we have seen, the House of Morgan got its start selling the bonds of American states and localities and their works to the British. At various points in history, foreign investors were substantial to majority owners of American municipal bonds.

That changed with the adoption of the income tax in the twentieth century, because municipals were deemed exempt from federal income tax, which meant they could attract investors with lower coupons than Treasury bonds. This explicit subsidy of the states by the federal government is meant to lower local borrowing costs, but it has had the effect of radically altering the municipal market. Investors to whom

---

[1] *Wall Street: A History*, by Charles R. Geisst. (New York, Oxford University Press, 1997, p. 159).

taxes do not matter, such as foreigners and most domestic institutional investors such as pension funds, have no interest in the market. Individuals, mutual funds, and bank trust departments representing them accounted for 77.5 percent of the $1.765 trillion municipal market in 2002, according to the Federal Reserve. The balance was owned principally by commercial banks and property-and-casualty insurance companies. This is one market where you have an advantage over Bill Gross: As an institutional manager, he has no interest in adding municipals to his portfolios unless they present extraordinary trading opportunities. As Gross and the other bond sharks take a pass on this market, if you are smart and willing to apply Total Return principles, you can dive in and make money.

Today's municipal market is dominated not by canals and turnpikes but by general obligation bonds, education issues, health care facilities, pollution controls, and public-sanitation and water-supply debt. Before 1986, a growing segment of the market was devoted to industrial development, but abuses in that sector—essentially using tax-free status to underwrite commercial construction—led to changes in federal tax law that disallowed deductibility for such special commercial uses. Today, municipal industrial bonds are a tiny segment of the market. Most of it is high-quality debt, but municipals are not immune to risk. New York City went broke in 1975 and Orange County, California, in 1994. In 2003, municipal markets were roiled by a judicial decision in tiny Madison County, Illinois, where a local judge awarded a multibillion dollar settlement to tort lawyers against Philip Morris Companies that threatened to unravel the Master Settlement Agreement (MSA) between the tobacco industry and states' attorneys-general. Numerous states, including California and New Jersey, had issued municipal bonds that would be repaid from future revenues from the $368.5 billion MSA. At one point, California shelved $2.3 billion in tobacco bonds that it had planned to issue to fight its budget crisis. Virginia, another beneficiary of the MSA, jerked a $767 million bond issue that underwriters had already priced; that is, for which they had already lined up customers.

The tobacco brouhaha was one of the biggest reasons the municipal market was battered in 2003, but there were many others, notably the general economic weakness—akin to credit risk—that made it more difficult for states to service their bonds. General obligation bonds typically mandate bond servicing, even if taxes have to be raised as a result, but the nation was in an anti-tax mood. Even the liberal state of Oregon was unable to push through a tax increase, and the equally liberal citizens of the Seattle, Washington, rejected the proposed "Java Tax" on triple lattes. It was not that investors worried that states would actually go broke and completely default on their bond obligations. The perception was instead that, like a dicey government in the Third World, states would temporarily refuse to service interest payments due on their bonds.

Because of the worry over credit, according to Morningstar Inc., the average municipal bond fund managed to eke out gains of only 0.48 percent in the first eight months of the year, after racking up total returns the prior year of nearly 8 percent. The prior two times the group had done so badly, with mid single-digit losses in 1994 and 1999, short-term interest rates had been rising, but that was not the case in 2003. Rather, it was tobacco and burgeoning state budget woes that had saturated the limited market. Scrambling to meet soaring mandated costs like Medicaid with revenues tumbling along with employment, states had issued bonds in record amounts. The total was $290 billion in 2001 and $350 billion in 2002. The average in the prior decade had been $225 billion annually.

The market for municipal debt is limited not only by the absence of foreign buyers, but also by its intensely local nature. High-tax states and cities can wring lower yields from investors by making their bonds exempt from state and local, as well as federal, income tax. Income taxes on residents top out at 6.37 percent in New Jersey and 9.3 percent in California. Given the deductibility of state taxes by California and New Jersey taxpayers, their residents enjoy the greatest benefits of ownership, and offerings are priced accordingly. A dollar of fully taxable interest, such as that paid by corporate bonds, is worth only 61.4 cents to someone in the top federal tax bracket. It is worth only 52.1 cents to the beleaguered taxpayers of California, which jousts with Vermont to have the most onerous income-tax rates in the country. Therefore, everything else being equal, a tax-free bond would only have to yield 0.614 percent as much as a Treasury to attract investors nationally, and something more than 0.521 percent as much in California. (Because the interest is deductible on federal returns, the actual marginal tax rate is not the sum of the federal and local rate, but something less, depending on the amount of tax-free income.) In reality, municipal yields are almost never this low. For one thing, Treasury interest is deductible on state returns. For another, no municipal is as free of credit risk as a Treasury. And not all municipal bond buyers are in the top bracket. Historically, therefore, high-quality municipal bonds have traded at a smaller discount to Treasuries, somewhere within hailing distance of 0.85 percent for long-term debt. You watch: Municipals often come with some carry.

You can calculate the tax-equivalent yield of any municipal bond or fund with a simple formula. Subtract your marginal tax rate from 1.00; the result in the 35 percent federal bracket is 0.65. Divide this fraction into the municipal yield, expressed as a whole number, such as 4.00 (percent). The result is your personal taxable-equivalent yield.

Heavy issuance in 2001 and 2002 took advantage of interest rates that were steadily declining at the time. In ordinary circumstances, that situation would also lead to the municipal market's equivalent of a call on some of its outstanding debt. Calls are a prepayment option—the right to give investors back their money when interest rates are falling (when they least want it, of course). Municipalities accomplish something similar by performing what is called a pre-refunding or an advanced refunding. An escrow account is created to service the existing high-interest debt, and new bonds are issued sufficiently to buy enough Treasuries to pay off the old issue. The difference in yield between the old bonds and the new has the effect of reducing a locality's net debt burden—but it does not work when Treasury and municipal yields are the same. Refunding was a traditional borrowing window that snapped shut at the worst possible time. This had the benefit of insulating bond-holders from prepayment risk but because it forced states to stick to their interest obligations, it worsened the credit problem.

Many states are not permitted, under their constitutions, to run deficits and therefore they do not have the federal government's advantage of being able to maintain a current account deficit. The current account deficit represents the difference between total investment in the American enterprise and the portion of that amount that Americans themselves contribute. A deficit means capital is flowing into the country from abroad. Just as Europeans helped underwrite American railroads in the nineteenth century, citizens of the world are underwriting American technology and biomedical developments today—as well as the federal budget deficit. A third of all Treasury bonds are owned by foreign governments and their people. However, foreigners stay out of the municipal market: Why accept the lower interest when you do not get the tax advantages?

For that matter, most citizens do not buy munis, and for the same reason. Our principal investment accounts are our IRAs and 401(k)s, which are tax-deferred and therefore do not enjoy the tax benefits that come with municipals. It would be foolish to buy munis in a retirement account because all of its proceeds are taxed as ordinary income, including the money you had put in to buy the bonds. A responsible retirement-account trustee will not allow you to make such a mistake: They prohibit munis in any form, including mutual funds. (You could end-run this rule in some brokerage IRAs, as I explain, but you would not want to.) Munis are for your conventional, taxable investment portfolio.

With the supply of tax-free bonds exploding and demand constant, capitalism's invisible hand sent their price down and their yields up. This sent Bill Gross, in his personal portfolio, out buying munis. Specifically, he recommended closed-end muni-bond funds that use leverage to boost their yields even higher.

As I discussed in the previous chapter, closed-end funds, sometimes mistakenly called closed-end mutual funds, are bought and sold like stock—most are traded on the New York Stock Exchange—and buyers pay whatever the market will bear. (In an IRA or 401(k) that offers stock investments, you could conceivably buy a closed-end muni fund; it has a three-letter ticker symbol just like any exchange-listed stock. But, I repeat, you would not want to.) Closed-ends have fixed portfolios that make them easier to manage than open-end mutual funds; inflows and outflows do not exist. They also have the right to do something mutual funds cannot, which is to borrow assets and use them to lever up returns. They do this in a way that any state treasurer who has ever done a refunding can understand. They sell preferred shares in the fund to institutional investors, and invest the proceeds at rates higher than they are paying in interest on the preferred shares. Not all closed-ends are leveraged, and one reason is that not all managers are skillful enough to invest such monies profitably. Boosting returns by imaginative techniques, including leverage, are bread and butter at PIMCO, however, and it runs a small family of closed-end funds that (by no coincidence, I expect) meet the criteria Gross recommends.

There are hundreds of closed-end funds investing in everything from stocks to real estate. But among fixed-income funds, it is leverage that makes them potentially more appealing than mutual funds, and in the current market municipal closed-ends are most appealing of all, in Gross's view. So while books have been written about investing in closed-ends, the best way to broach the subject is in the context of municipal bonds.

There are nine muni-bond PIMCO funds: three sets of three, one investing in national bonds and two state-only portfolios—California and New York (see Table 6.1). All are managed by the same team, which is headed by Mark McCray, PIMCO's point-person on tax-free bonds. In each instance, the original portfolio was the first to be launched, followed by the others. PIMCO Municipal Income Fund, for example, was launched in June 2001. Muni Income II came out the following summer, and Muni Income III a few months later. Closed-ends cannot accept new contributions, except in special circumstances like so-called rights offerings to existing shareholders, so creating new portfolios

Table 6.1 PIMCO Municipal Bond Closed-End Funds

Fund	Premium/ Discount %	Yield % –1	Taxable- Equivalent Yield % –2
PIMCO Calif. Muni Income (PCQ)	3.29	6.27	11.26
PIMCO Calif. Muni Income II (PCK)	1.82	6.69	12.01
PIMCO Calif. Muni Income III (PZC)	2.96	6.58	11.81
PIMCO Muni Income (PMF)	4.63	6.54	10.06
PIMCO Muni Income II (PML)	2.34	6.82	10.49
PIMCO Muni Income III (PMX)	1.37	6.76	10.40
PIMCO N.Y. Muni Income (PNF)	5.61	6.21	10.68
PIMCO N.Y. Muni Income II (PNI)	3.70	6.57	11.30
PIMCO N.Y. Muni Income III (PYN)	0.34	6.55	11.26

Note: Premium/discount and yield statistics as of June 30, 2003. 1-Yield as percentage of market price. 2-Taxable-equivalent yield based on top federal (and state, as appropriate) income tax rate of 35 percent (California top rate 9.3 percent, New York 6.85 percent) for tax year 2003. Actual marginal state totals can be somewhat lower if the investor has a large amount of tax-free income, and yields therefore correspondingly less.
Source: ETFConnect.com, Federation of Tax Administrators

with similar characteristics is not unusual. But the numbered funds are not mere clones of their sibling. At the time of their March 31, 2003, portfolio reports, California Municipal Income II had a much longer duration (11.1 years) than the original, whose duration was 9.6 years. Municipal Income III at the time had a duration of 6.8 years. These durations fall into the "long" category, as opposed to the "intermediate."

At the end of the second quarter of 2003, all of these funds were trading at premiums to their net asset value (NAV). Premiums and discounts are both the bane and the boon of the closed-end universe. Mutual funds always trade at NAV; they satisfy supply and demand by issuing new shares or redeeming old ones. Closed-ends cannot, so demand quickly translates into share price. The rich yields of the PIMCO funds—a taxable-equivalent yield around 10 percent for the national fund and 11 percent for the state portfolios—were worth something extra on that snapshot date of June 30, but sentiment is fickle. Those premiums contracted the following month, and on July 25, PIMCO California Municipal Income's premium had been erased by a 3.15 percent discount, boosting its yield to 7.02 percent and the taxable equivalent to an eye-popping 12.60 percent. The same thing is true of closed-ends issued by other vendors, and they are abundant. PIMCO for decades focused strictly on its institutional business and got into the fund business relatively recently. Many other fund complexes, notably John Nuveen and BlackRock, offer closed-end municipal bond funds.

Yields like that are redolent of junk bonds, but these funds invest in anything but: 48 percent of the bonds owned by California Municipal Income were rated Triple-A, as of its report dated March 31, 2003. PIMCO's approach in its muni funds, says McCray, "is to focus on high-quality essential services or general-obligation debt." Even McCray's tobacco bonds were more conservative than most: They had a so-called turbo-redemption feature that reduced their effective life to 10 or 12 years from 30 or 40, eliminating a huge portion of their risk.

Not that leveraged closed-end funds are themselves a low-risk investment: Just as borrowing benefits a fund when it is rising, it punishes when it declines. Between September 9, 2002, and June 30, 2003, as the muni market swooned, the share price of PIMCO California Municipal Income declined 80 cents, to $14.55 from $15.35. This is a drop of 5.2 percent, which more than erased the 77 cents of dividends it yielded during the period. The net effect was that in a 10-month span, an investment in the fund returned slightly less than nothing. So timing a purchase of a leverage closed-end fund can have an even greater impact on its return than is true of investments in general.

Although PIMCO has many competitors in the closed-end business, it distinguishes itself in part by offering extremely low fees. Penny for penny, fees subtract from total returns. The total charges on PIMCO's closed-end municipal funds is 0.45 percent of assets. Sponsors who charge higher fees are either going to deliver lower returns, or they are going to be forced to invest in riskier securities. Bill Gross is one of the mutual fund industry's most vociferous advocates for low-fee funds. Fees are important in all forms of investing, but particularly in the single-digit world of fixed income. Municipals, the lowest-yielding bonds, are the most vulnerable to the wealth-robbing effects of high annual expenses.

Closed-end funds do not exhaust the options open to municipal bond investors, of course. Virtually any brokerage firm can sell you individual municipals, and this is the way most investors own them. A time-tested strategy for smoothing out the effects of fluctuations in interest rates is to construct a ladder of bonds that mature annually over the next 10 years. Until funds are needed, maturing bonds are replaced with others maturing 10 years hence, so the ladder is perpetual. Constructing such a ladder requires diligence, however, because it adds individual security risk to all the others. Many municipal bonds are insured, but that only covers the principal—not interest—and insurance companies themselves are not immune to failure. Buying insured bonds adds another layer of due diligence you need to perform—the insurer as well as the insured.

As simple and elegant as bond ladders are, they are not perfect investment platforms. This is the investment model that Gross's total return approach has bettered since he began implementing it in the early 1970s. An actively managed bond portfolio can reflect strategic decisions about the relative merits of sectors within the municipal market that affect current as well as planned holdings. And buying a portfolio of individual bonds can be expensive. Even those that do not carry explicit sales charges have them buried somewhere within the price; how else could brokerage firms make a profit? The various fees and commissions buried within a bond can amount to as much as 4 percent of its price. Some securities firms offer separate-account programs which provide customized portfolios of individual bonds for an annual fee, with minimums as low as $250,000 or even $100,000. As with funds, however, fees matter greatly in this arena, as well. Every fraction of a percentage point paid in fees is one deducted from total returns.

Another disadvantage of individual bonds—which is true of closed-ends, although to a different degree—is that their flow of income, unless it is consumed, can be difficult to manage. The annual revenue stream of even $100,000 in bonds, a modest individual portfolio, can be insufficient to buy another bond. This is yet another disadvantage that individual investors face compared with Gross, managing his billions. You sometimes have to do tricky math work, adding to the separate account, to ensure it remains entirely in bonds—or withdraw cash regularly from it, skewing your asset allocation.

Closed-end funds are somewhat different in this regard: The PIMCO funds pay distributions monthly, whereas bonds pay semiannually. But individual closed-end shares are much cheaper than bonds, meaning proceeds can be more easily deployed into more shares than into more bonds. Even this involves commissions, however, and when cash yields are low, as they were at the time of writing, the inability to invest these fractional flows efficiently constitutes what economists call an "opportunity cost." The one investment that ameliorates this cost is the conventional mutual fund. It offers automatic reinvestment of dividends and other distributions at the fund's then-current net asset value. In most investment arenas, dividend reinvestment entails paying taxes on these uncollected proceeds, but tax-free municipals escape even this inconvenience.

Mutual funds are something of a basket of options themselves, but most work in favor of shareholders. There is the option to put money in and take it out at will, although with load funds this can engender sales charges. Purchases and redemptions are made at net asset value. Portfolios are professionally managed and thoroughly diversified. They are unleveraged, so debt is no burden when markets move down. Far more information is widely available about mutual funds than either closed-ends or individual bonds. For most individuals who have a portfolio of their core fixed-income portfolio in municipals (which is discussed in the final chapter), mutual funds are superior to closed-ends because their risks are less.

PIMCO operates mutual funds analogous, but not identical, to its roster of closed-end funds. PIMCO California Intermediate Municipal Bond Fund had a duration of 4.8 years as of March 31, 2003. The duration of its long equivalent, PIMCO California Municipal Bond Fund, was 8.0 years. The family's other mutual funds include PIMCO Municipal Bond, PIMCO Short-Duration Municipal Income, and PIMCO New York Municipal Bond. As in closed-ends, PIMCO is a relative newcomer to municipal mutual funds; none of the portfolios has been around 10 years. There are, however, literally hundreds of such funds from other fund families, including state-only portfolios for a number of other states, such as Florida, New Jersey, Pennsylvania, and North Carolina. All or nearly all are tracked and rated by firms like Morningstar Inc. and Lipper Inc., and many are individually followed by analysts from those and other firms. There are also a host of online sources of fund information. One of the most provocative web sites is called *FundAlarm.com*. The operator, Roy Weitz, is a curmudgeon who takes advantage of the fact that most of the financial media highlight funds to buy. He focuses on funds to sell, and keeps a roster of them called 3-Alarm Funds. These are funds that have underperformed their benchmarks for one, three, and five years. As of September 30, 2003, there were no PIMCO bond funds on that list.

PIMCO invests in municipal markets as it does everywhere else, primarily driven by the firm's secular vision of markets over the next three to five years. "That's not to say that we do not react on a daily basis," says McCray, because PIMCO trades heavily around its central themes, always laboring to eke out the extra 50 to 100 basis points (hundredths of a percentage point) it strives to deliver for investors. And PIMCO's secular outlook for municipals is very favorable. "The things that have caused municipals to underperform, to become a relatively cheap asset class, are things that secularly we think will tend to favor municipal bonds," McCray says. Chief among these are the states' budget difficulties. As state finances deteriorated, PIMCO stuffed its municipal portfolios with bonds of the highest credit quality it could find. It drastically reduced its exposure to tobacco early in 2003. But the lingering employment recession that began in 2001 is slowly leading to widespread recovery, and McCray believes credit quality overall will improve substantially in coming years. One of the factors underpinning higher Treasury yields—the linchpin to which all credits relate—was their relative scarcity amid budget surpluses. Those have been transformed into deficits, meaning fresh debt will be issued and more of the market's demand supplied. The federal government, fighting economic weakness, is also laboring to hold down short-term rates. Together these trends should help push down muni yields and thus allow the price of muni bonds, which is the reciprocal of their yield, to rise. So PIMCO is holding tight to high quality and shortening duration of its municipal portfolios, but is prepared to lengthen duration and dip into weaker bonds as credit conditions improve.

The performance of municipal mutual funds turns on two key issues: management and fees. You want the best of the former and the lowest of the latter. Fortunately, with literally hundreds of funds to choose from the choices are abundant, and hardly limited to PIMCO. Analytical tools are abundant as well. I would be remiss not to plug CNBC on MSN Money, for which I am the mutual funds columnist. Its research tools have consistently attracted favorable reviews from the likes of *Barron's* and *Forbes*.

Federal Reserve Chairman Alan Greenspan rattled bond markets in early summer when he made clear the central bank will tolerate inflation, which implies higher long-term rates, and indeed the market's reaction promptly created them. But PIMCO's view is that Fed expansionism is only relative, intended to combat deflation; it has no desire to choke off economic recovery with substantially higher borrowing costs. "Certainly higher interest rates from the Fed would nip recovery in the bud," McCray says. The combination of stronger bond issuers and a rein, albeit loose, on rates is like a greenhouse over tempest-tossed municipal bonds.

In summary, you should exercise some care when you include municipal bonds in your portfolio. Consider them for your nest egg— an idea I explore in more detail in Chapter Nine. Simultaneously, consider taking advantage of them by buying funds, individual issues, or closed-end funds, for trading purposes.

CHAPTER 7

Where the "Oh, Boys!" Are

The United States is by far the world's largest economy, with a gross domestic product of nearly $10 trillion. The American economy is also far more vibrant than any other developed nation. Domestic GDP grew at a 3.1 percent annual rate in the 1990s, compared with 2.1 percent in Great Britain and 1.8 percent in Germany, France, and Japan.

Taken together, however, the other great developed nations are a bigger market than our own. Japan's GDP is nearly $4.9 trillion. Germany's is nearly $1.9 trillion, the United Kingdom's $1.4 trillion, and France's $1.3 trillion. Probability alone would suggest that investment opportunities exist elsewhere among these mighty powers, and of course they do. This is especially true of fixed-income investments. Anemic economies are under pressure to lower rather than raise interest rates, which boosts bond prices. In the second quarter of 2003, France's gross domestic contracted 0.3 percent. It was the worst one-quarter showing since 1993. The GDP of Germany, Europe's current "sick man," owing in part to the absorption of the former East Germany, was little changed. For bond investors, though, "Eurosclerosis" is an opportunity, not a bugbear.

Japan is a singular exception: The overnight borrowing rate there is 0.06 percent, effectively zero. On average, inflation in Japan was entirely absent during the 1990s, and in 2001 consumer prices actually declined 0.7 percent. Rates are so low that there are simply next to no opportunities in Japan. In the United States, meanwhile, growth was 2.4 percent, but by historical standards this is tepid. In the seven calendar quarters following the formal end of recession in the fall of 2001, U.S. GDP growth averaged 2.6 percent; in the corresponding periods after prior recessions it averaged 5.4 percent, according to research by Morgan Stanley.

These are a few of the "wet logs" Bill Gross fears will hobble the Federal Reserve's efforts to reflate the American economy, and will also constrain the other key economies so much that global commerce will sputter instead of catching fire. As a matter of fact, the Fed is the only central bank in the world with an expansionary agenda. Japanese officials fret about deflation, but have only recently done anything about it. The European Central Bank cut interest rates in June, at the same time as the Fed, but to 2.0 percent. In Great Britain, short-term rates are 3.5 percent. These nations remain avowedly determined to fight the battle against rising prices that the United States has declared to be over and won. They do not find the Fed's position persuasive; U.S. inflation has long tended to run a half to three-quarters of a percentage point higher than continental Europe's. America's worst modern inflation, in the 1960s and 1970s, was trivial compared with inflation in Germany during the 1920s, when Deutsche marks were carried not in wallets but in baskets.

Gross notes that there are structural impediments to growth in continental Europe and Japan. Economies are stagnant because their populations are aging; they were on the losing side of World War Two and never had a baby boom, and thus no echo boom. Aging populations are savers, not spenders, inhibiting growth. And they are not even saving enough: Looming pension crises are worse overseas than at home. Other developed countries are much less tolerant of immigrants than the United States; Japan is xenophobic. European economies are also much more dependent on manufacturing than the United States, in an era when manufacturing jobs are moving even from Korea to China. U.S.-style deregulation has been largely shunned. Labor markets are rigid. Hiring a worker in Germany is tantamount to guaranteeing a lifetime job and a lush retirement, so job creation is exported to Shanghai and North Carolina. Taxes are crushingly high to fund such social benefits as unemployment checks that are paid for years. Economic mobility is frozen: Whereas an American moving from Alabama, say, to St. Louis to find work is not out of the ordinary, the idea of a Sardinian moving to Paris for the same reason is all but absurd. Protectionism is rampant: Despite the World Trade Organization (WTO) and the European Community (EC), domestic industries are sheltered from Joseph Schumpeter's "creative destruction." When the French shipyard building the world's largest cruise ship, the Alstom SA engineering group, lurched toward bankruptcy, the French government bailed it out for $3.2 billion, nationalizing 31.5 percent of it, the maximum its own laws allowed. Japan has been nationalizing its banks, in the same quasi-socialist hope that taxpayer money will effect a miracle that private capital could not. Competitiveness lags: Especially in Europe, corporations are years behind the United States in cutting costs and rebuilding their balance sheets, and they get little support from their governments or the European Union (EU) in terms of stimulative fiscal or monetary policies. Indeed, the EU's own Stability Pact inhibits its members from stimulating their economies (in the name of inflation control) with government deficits. (It is routinely violated, but nothing on the scale of U.S. budget deficits.) Interest rates are so stubbornly high in Great Britain, PIMCO's Sudi Mariappa says, because the Bank of England, like many European central banks, has official inflation targets to which it hews. The Federal Reserve does not announce such targets, although it certainly pays attention to inflation trends. The bottom line, says Mariappa, is "they foresee higher inflation than we do."

As if that were not enough, the U.S. dollar has weakened more than 15 percent against the currencies of its major trading partners, making them less competitive globally. Economists have been predicting such a break for years: The U.S. current account deficit, already 5 percent of GDP and headed toward 6 percent, represents IOUs written to foreigners that are not redeemed only because the dollar is the world's reserve currency. The dollar has declined because foreign confidence is ebbing; the break would have been worse except for serious efforts by foreign nations to defend their own currencies. In the first half of 2003, Japan's central bank bought $50 billion worth of dollars, trying to halt the dollar's slide against the yen. Lee Thomas III, the PIMCO managing director who focuses on international portfolio strategy for the firm, says, "It takes between $1 billion and $2 billion of foreign money flowing into the U.S. each day to keep the dollar afloat." This is not, he wryly adds, a trend that can be sustained forever, particularly when U.S. securities, such as its bonds, become less attractive as their prices fall. The price of the 10-year Treasury fell 10 percent in June and July, and foreigners are the most likely, not the least, to withdraw from an adverse U.S. bond market. Much of the flows come from foreign banks, which find few good borrowers domestically, owing to their poor economies, and so venture into the U.S. market. PIMCO attributes a significant portion of the June–July rout to this kind of foreign selling because it was concentrated in the two groups (Treasuries and agencies) in which foreigners own more than one-third of the market.

All of this is enough to excite a bond investor's animal spirits.

Gloom is gold under the perpetual cloud that overhangs the fixed-income world. Gross believes that European government bonds and

Figure 7.1   U.S. Current Account Balance, 1960–2003

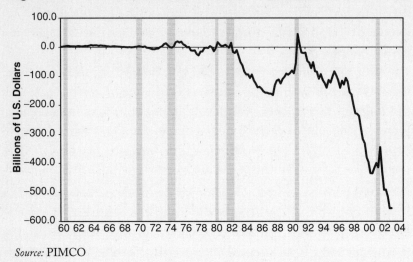

Source: PIMCO

certain Japanese bonds will outperform domestic issues in coming years. They are attractive, he says, both on their merits and as a play on the dollar. "International holdings denominated in foreign currencies" is one of his favorite investment ideas although, as explained in Chapter Eight, PIMCO Total Return Fund by policy hedges currency risk, and thus cannot participate in the dollar weakness Gross expects.

Fundamentally, PIMCO expects European interest rates to continue to decline. Further declines in the United States are not expected. Lower rates mean higher bond prices. Most of the value is concentrated in bonds with short maturities. In mid-August, for example, the spread to Treasuries—that is, the premium over the yield of the corresponding U.S. government bond—was 292 basis points for two-year Australian bonds, 172 points for the five-year maturity, and 102 points for 10-year notes.

All of Europe's major nations are sporting relatively lush yields. The two-year spread for German bunds is 77 basis points. For Italy, it is 83; Canada, 119; the United Kingdom, 226. The spreads diminish at longer maturities: On five-year notes, Germany's bonds yield an additional 8 basis points, and Italy's 9. On 10-year notes, while spreads remain positive for Canadian, Australian, and British bonds, in Germany they are 29 points below the U.S. level, and in Italy 14 points.

As an institutional investor, PIMCO does enjoy one big advantage over individuals like you or me: It can buy foreign bonds in the form of futures contracts known as interest-rate swaps, which have a yield premium built into them. Two-year Australian swaps trade at a premium of 330 points over Australia's bonds themselves, a gain of 38 basis points, or $3/8$ percent. Swaps are an enormous market—bigger than bonds themselves in the United States and 10 times bigger in Europe. The contracts typically begin at $5 million, however, so aside from the super rich it is strictly a professional's game. It helps explain, however, how PIMCO bond funds can wring enough extra yield out of their investments that they can pay all of their own expenses and still deliver a percentage point of excess returns to shareholders.

The swap market works as a normalizer of interest rates, so they can be conveniently compared against each other. The baseline for comparison is the London Interbank Offered Rate, or LIBOR. It is currently slightly higher than similar yields in the United States. The six-month rate is 1.19 percent. The rate for one year is 1.40 percent, and for 10 years 4.95 percent. Swap contracts essentially create a fixed-rate bond out of a floating-rate interest market. When used in conjunction with bonds themselves, they neutralize interest-rate risk. For example, a 10-year swap currently yields 4.95 percent. A corresponding U.S. Treasury yields 4.50 percent. You buy the bond and sell the swap. You invest the proceeds in the six-month LIBOR market. You pay the buyer of the swap semiannual interest at the annual rate of 4.95 percent. You have actually earned, however, 5.69 percent—4.5 percent on the bond and 1.19 percent on LIBOR. You receive the premium because all of the interest-rate risk is on your side—the buyer gets 4.95 percent whether LIBOR goes to 10 percent or to zero. Swap yields are generally positive over corresponding bond yields, but as the 10-year example above shows, they can be negative. Buyers and sellers are constantly juggling their views on interest rates when they enter into swaps, because the wrong bet could erase profits on either side.

In the case of interest rates at the moment, however, individual American investors should be willing to accept rate risk on foreign government bonds, PIMCO believes, because their rates are more likely than ours to decline, handing the investor a capital gain. Similarly, it is more likely that the dollar will depreciate against foreign currencies than it will appreciate, so unhedged foreign bonds are best of all. As a practical matter, a purchase of a foreign bond in inherently unhedged; hedges are built in separate securities on the futures market. If you buy a British bond for £1000, you will pay for it with dollars converted at the prevailing rate, which now is $1.61 per pound sterling. Your total investment is $1,610. If you sell it in two years with a gain of 5 percent, which is a price of £1050, and sterling has appreciated 5 percent against the dollar (meaning the conversion rate is $1.69), your return is $1,774.50—a profit of $164.50, or 4.98 percent a year. In addition, you would have received the bond's coupon (4.10 percent) translated into dollars at whatever rate prevailed every six months. The total return over two years would be more than 9 percent. Animal spirits, indeed, for a bond with no credit risk. Not that the interest-rate and currency risks are trivial. But you have accepted them because of your confidence that, within two years, both British rates and the U.S. dollar would be lower. If you are wrong on one score, but not the other, you would still have received more than you could on a two-year Treasury. Only if you are wrong on both do you stand to lose. In short, the odds are on your side (see Figure 7.2).

Even in beleaguered Japan, PIMCO is finding attractive investments, although in the private sector. In July, the island nation's fourth-largest bank, UFJ, issued subordinated debt in the United States. Japan's banks are basket cases, victims of crony capitalism at its near-worst. They underwrote the fantastic expansion Japan enjoyed in the 1980s, when its economy seemed poised to topple all the other great nations and it was buying up foreign properties as if the yen were

Figure 7.2   Dollar versus Pound Sterling, 1994–2003

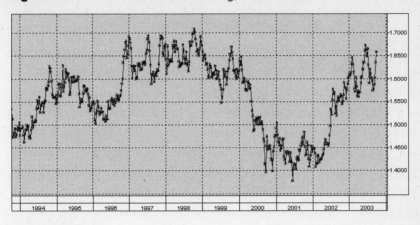

Source: PIMCO

Monopoly® money. Americans will remember that two of the worst such investments were the purchase on the East Coast of Rockefeller Center and on the West of the Pebble Beach golf course, each at exorbitant prices that were later bought back by Americans for perhaps 50 cents on the dollar. Domestically, however, foolish property loans of the 1980s, many of them in default by U.S. standards, remain on the books, a hollowing out of the financial system whose magnitude is almost beyond comprehension. At the peak of Japanese arrogance, its own real estate was trading hands at prices that valued the nation's property more highly than all of the United States, which is 25 times larger. America's own version of a property bubble, the savings and loan crisis of the late 1980s, cost taxpayers $132 billion and was erased within a few years. Japan's many fewer taxpayers are paying vastly more in dribbles and drabs; many of UFJ's competitors have been nationalized, making their bond investors whole at the public's expense.

Despite this history, and indeed in part because of it, the UFJ deal caught Bill Gross's eye. A nation willing to nationalize its banks—and not by confiscating them—was implicitly attaching its own risk-free credit status to the paper. The bonds were yielding, moreover, 280 basis points more than Treasuries. Gross's investment committee summoned the firm's Japan strategist, Tomoya Masanao, to make a presentation on the credit. Its members could find no flaw in the deal sufficient to offset the considerable interest-rate bonus it paid. When Resona Bank was recapitalized the prior month, subordinated debt holders were made whole. The same thing had happened with two other banks.

PIMCO began buying the bonds, and within a month, other investors were reaching the same conclusion and the bonds traded up to a spread of 250 points. This was not a major bet—the bonds PIMCO Total Return Fund acquired amounted to less than half a percent of its total portfolio. Gross's major bets usually involve big-picture matters like interest rates. Bets on individual securities are diversified very thoroughly, to insulate the portfolio for mistakes, which are inevitable. An individual, however, following Gross's total return approach could have made a major bet on the bonds. One tenet of his investment philosophy is to make bold moves when the odds are on his side. These bonds were not hard to buy; they are so liquid that they are included in a Lehman Brothers U.S. bond index.

If the developed world has fallen into a slow-growth malaise, the developing world has not. China's real GDP growth in the 1990s was an astonishing 9.8 percent annually. Singapore's rate was 7.8 percent, Malaysia 7.2 percent, South Korea 6.4 percent, Chile 6.3 percent, India 5.5 percent, Thailand 5.0 percent, Hong Kong 4.3 percent, and Mexico 3.6 percent. Russia's GDP grew 6.9 percent in 2002. Hungary, Poland, the Czech Republic, Mexico, and Brazil all grew faster in 2002 than Great Britain, Europe's strongest economy. The population of the developing world is much younger than that of the developed West and is growing much faster. Secular trends promise to further enrich these markets. The United Nations projects that Europe's population will decline by 5 percent by the year 2030, and more than 20 percent of the population of Germany, Russia, the United Kingdom, and Australia will be over 65. In Japan and Italy, nearly 30 percent of the population will be aged. In the developing world, however, populations are growing rapidly, adding young workers and consumers; the fastest growth in total employment is expected to come in Asia and Latin America. Citizens of less-developed countries also save much more aggressively than Westerners. China's savings rate of 43 percent of GDP is the highest in the world, but Hong Kong, India, Indonesia, Korea, and Malaysia are not far behind. In the United States, savings are 16 percent of GDP.

Despite high savings rates, however, developing nations are dependent on the developed world for capital. The sum of all these trends is a prescription for higher investment profits than in the developed world, and profits indeed have been lush. In the 12 months ended August 21, 2003, emerging markets bonds rose in value by 30.09 percent in U.S. dollar terms.

Emerging markets bonds, according to Lehman Brothers, comprise a total market place of about $250 billion. They have maturities of about 11 years and durations just under six. They yield about 8.2 percent (comparable to domestic high-yield bonds), which is an average spread to Treasuries of 425 basis points. Spreads vary by issuer, of course. Argentine bonds, whose economy is in shambles, have a spread of 1466 points, which effectively means they do not trade at all. Brazil, whose spread was more than 2000 points in October 2002, has contracted to 640 as the West has discovered its left-leaning president is not nearly as radical as had been feared. Mexico's spread is only 225 points, not much higher than high-quality American corporate bonds, and Russia's is 260. In Thailand the spread is only 180 points, and in emerging Europe in the 320-point range. Contracting spreads are a sign of improving credit quality. Mohamed El-Erian, PIMCO's chief of emerging markets, notes that the average credit quality of the group has improved to about the Double-B range, and more than 40 percent of issuers qualify for investment-grade ratings, including Mexico, Poland, South Korea, Malaysia, Chile, and South Africa.

These bonds are primarily the sovereign debt of developing nations, issued internationally and denominated in dollars, euros or yen. Corporate debt is rare, only about 10 percent of the total. Private issuers are more likely to sell stock than bonds, because of their weak financials.

This market has come a long way in since the day of Brady bonds. These were originally issued as part of Mexico's debt crisis in 1994. Brady bonds, named for former Treasury Secretary Nicholas Brady, carried guarantees of the U.S. government, backing about one-third of the total value of each issue. This potential liability attracted controversy at the time but proved not to matter; the guarantees were remarkably successful because the issuing nations were extremely diligent in adhering to accounting standards and fundamental economic reforms that underlay the loans. Other nations in Latin America subsequently did Brady bond deals and they became a standard means by which developing nations with doubtful credit histories could access global capital markets. Today, Brady bonds are no longer being issued and account for only 11.16 percent of the Lehman Brothers Emerging Markets Bond Index. However, one of their legacies, particularly after the "Asian contagion" of 1997, has been far greater transparency in accounting and other financial information. The lack of it was the prime cause of the contagion, which led institutional investors to shun the entire group for a time. They have since returned, however, and flows of funds into developing economies have accelerated.

By the same token, structural impediments to foreign investments in developing markets remain. Institutions, such as political organization, legal systems, financial controls, and public oversight, are fragile. "You've got to monitor developments on a daily basis," says El-Erian, whose staff distributes a morning report every day to PIMCO's portfolio managers and partners. Fund flows are fragile, too, less easily spooked than in 1997 but quick to flee at the first sign of peril. Taken together, fixed-income investors constitute what Bill Gross calls the bond market's "vigilantes," expressing their disapproval of a government or a corporation by dumping its bonds en masse. Information that would have taken months to reach British investors in American railroads in the nineteenth century reaches El-Erian's desk—and a similar one in his home—at light speed. Especially among institutions, some percentage of assets is typically dedicated to emerging markets as an asset class, and funds are moved within the pool but not in and out. The majority of emerging markets investments, however, are made opportunistically. For example, El-Erian says, "People can invest in Ford [Motor], but Mexico might offer better returns right now than Ford. So the dedicated portion is actually small relative to the crossover portion, so this asset class is exposed to developments in other, competing asset classes."

Yet another vulnerability these markets have is to their more-developed neighbors. If you are attracted to Polish government bonds but are concerned about Germany's weak economy, Poland is suddenly much less attractive, because its economy is heavily reliant on its vastly richer neighbor. "Every day, we make a decision: First fundamentals, second neighborhood," El-Erian says.

El-Erian's approach to investing in these markets is to view them as three separate buckets, each contributing to total returns in different ways. The first, and largest, is investment-grade credits in nations like Mexico and South Africa, where institutions are strengthening and political risk is moderate. The second, which he calls his "return engine," is credits like Brazil that give a lot more spread, although at the expense of more risk. The third he labels "intensive care credits," such as those of Argentina. When PIMCO sees no immediate prospect of meaningful recovery, these markets are shunned entirely. When it begins to suspect the patient is improving, however, it will begin taking small positions, which increase as its confidence builds. This is the tack PIMCO took when Brazil itself was still in intensive care in 2002. It did not invest significantly in the country until its new president enunciated, and began implementing, policies that made clear he recognized the importance of foreign investors and was willing to protect their property rights.

Lee Thomas, in a recent Global Markets Watch column, gave what he called his "first-ever book plug"—*Adventure Capitalist: The Ultimate Road Trip* by Jim Rogers (Random House, 2003). Rogers, a former hedge fund manager, trekked the world in a custom-made, mustard-yellow Mercedes. "It is unusual to find an experienced investor," Thomas wrote, "who will take the time to get to know foreign economies from the bottom up. And it is even more unusual to find one who can write with wit, clarity and solid economic reasoning."

Foreign bonds, from both the established and the emerging markets, offer great opportunities to Total Return investors. In the final third of the book, I explain how to duplicate Gross's approach with a core portfolio of bonds and a flexible portfolio. Trading foreign bonds presents the easiest way to add risk and return to your portfolio; swooping in and out of the foreign markets is an educated person's game, but if you can assemble your own "team" of secular advisers and keep track of events from Athens to Zagreb, you will be playing Gross's game and reaping his rewards.

PART THREE

The Royal Approach

CHAPTER 8

How to Invest
for the Next
Five Years

The genius of Bill Gross, from the gaming tables to the high-tech world of bond trading, is in knowing, quantifying, and playing risk. As you have learned from this book, Gross divides up the trends taking place in the world into cyclical and secular phenomena. He examines in a deep and searching way the relationship between cyclical and secular factors and the variables that operate in the bond universe: interest rate risk, credit risk, liquidity risk, currency risk, prepayment risk, and all of the other risks that can affect bond pricing. What Gross is trying to do is to calculate how the cyclical and secular factors affect all of these variables. As cyclical factors often cannot be predicted, he spends most of his time anticipating secular trends and analyzing whether or not they decrease or increase all of the risks that determine bond pricing.

In the next chapter, I show readers how to think like Bill Gross— how you can learn to anticipate and predict secular trends and trade your bond portfolio to take advantage of that. Before we discover how you can develop your own secular analysis, and Total Return strategy, I will reveal what Bill himself believes to be happening now. As a reader of this book you will have access to incredibly privileged, valuable information: Bill's current secular analysis, the thinking underpinning his bond trades in the fall of 2003. I had the privilege of spending time with him during 2003, collecting his thoughts about the coming movements in the bond markets. What are his views, his predictions of the secular factors likely to dominate the credit markets over the next five years?

Before revealing Bill's thoughts, I should remind readers that, in the time between my interview with him and this book's publication, new information may have come to light that disproves his current opinions. Bill would be the first to agree that this is, if not very likely, at least even odds. This is one reason why accomplished bond investors need to keep alert and engaged with the world—Total Return trading is not an area of investing in which you can make a five-year plan, stick with it, and come out on top. That said, Gross is renowned for his incredible eye. In the way a top fashion designer can see a coming trend by looking at the styles people wear in downtown New York, Bill can spot the wave-like movements of the world economy and the transformations coming years down the line. If you want to opportunistically play the bond market like Gross does, you will need to develop this sort of eye yourself, and you should aim to revise your secular analysis whenever conditions change—on a dime, if necessary. You must keep on top of a large flow of information, revising your own opinions regularly, estimating the future secular trends that will change our economy.

The Bond King's View

Certain broad secular trends emerge from the information Bill Gross has marshaled and implemented in his portfolios today. Together, they signal the end to the 20-plus year bull market that ended with the bursting of the Treasury bubble in the summer of 2003. Investors take bull markets for granted, but this one was historic. When it began, Treasury bills were yielding 15.5 percent and home mortgages cost as much as 17 percent. Now Treasuries have come down below 5 percent, and mortgages to 6 percent. These are rates that prevailed two generations ago, and a duplication of this experience is unlikely for decades to come, if ever.

Central banks, including the Federal Reserve and the European Central Bank, have developed potent policy weapons to prevent runaway inflation. Although the Fed is currently actually encouraging inflation, its goal is very mild price increases. Gross estimates that U.S. inflation is likely to average 3 percent in the coming five years, up from 2 percent or less in the last five. "That doesn't suggest Armageddon for the bond market," Gross notes. "It doesn't suggest anywhere close to the 1970s when they called bonds 'certificates of confiscation.'" That said, however, it is the *direction* of interest rates, rather than their absolute level, that drives the bond market. In the 1980s and 1990s that direction was down. Now it is up.

The direction of interest rates is up because the Fed, mindful of Japan's failed efforts to combat deflation, has switched its policy emphasis in an almost unprecedented way. "Central banks have almost always viewed inflation as the enemy, but in this case (the Fed) spoke to reflation as their target," Gross says. "It is very strange for a central bank to have reflation as a central goal, and that to me spoke of the end of the bull market in bonds." Gross believes the abrupt rise in the yield of the 10-year Treasury, from 3.11 percent in June to 4.41 percent at the end of July, 2003, could be followed, probably in 2004, with further increases to the range of 5 percent or a bit more. He is not concerned about rate increases beyond this range because, he notes, "It is not all clear sailing for reflation."

Reflation, in Gross's view, is hampered by the "wet logs" that exist in the world economy, pushing overall prices down. Global competition, epitomized by China and India, remains a powerful deflationary force.

Huge levels of private and public debt—including a federal deficit in the current fiscal year of more than $400 billion, with future deficits inevitable—weigh down spending "like the 16 tons that Tennessee Ernie Ford sang about," Gross says. Demographic trends contribute to these drags in two important ways. For one, baby boomers are buying fewer hot cars and putting more money into their retirement accounts, damping down consumer spending. For another, the aging of the population in the developed world is putting huge strains on pension systems, particularly in Europe; in Italy, for example, it is possible to retire before age 50 at 90 percent of terminal pay. Politicians have been reluctant even to recognize these trends because voters ignore them; it is such a serious problem that, in Germany, some advocate changing the voting system so that minor children get a vote, cast by their parents, so that younger, working people will be able to outvote retirees, who refuse to allow any changes in the pension system. Indeed, strikes over pension benefits have toppled political leaders in Europe. Domestically, Congress and President Bush are falling over each other in a rush to write a virtual blank check for retirees' prescription drugs. "It is not inevitable that Greenspan & Co. and the federal government through its budget deficits will be successful in reflating the U.S. economy," Gross warns. The stronger economy, expanding profit margins, lower unemployment and "the benefit at the polls that this brings with it...is not a slam dunk....The eventual inflationary fire will be a pretty mild one, as opposed to a bonfire."

Gross further believes that there are hidden risks to American bonds based on the strength of the U.S. dollar. For many years, it was quite strong relative to the British pound, the euro, and the Japanese yen. Foreign investors capitalized on this strength by purchasing enormous amounts of U.S. bonds. Currently non-U.S. investors own 35 percent of all outstanding Treasury bonds and 23 percent of domestic corporates. The dollar was not their only motivation. Treasuries are universally regarded as immune to risk, aside from interest rates, and interest rates in the United States, though relatively low by historical standards, were higher than in many developed nations, notably Japan. Although American corporations have taken a black eye in the press lately, they remain among the best managed and most profitable in the world. But currency risk remains in the background, and with the euro and the yen rallying in double digits against the dollar, that risk for foreigners is increasing. If they were to sell U.S. bonds, the impact on the market could be dramatic. They would not even have to desert U.S. corporations to do so: General Motors (GM) sells bonds in Europe, whose principal and interest are denominated in euros.

Indeed, PIMCO's investment committee recently asked the firm's foreign bond desk to investigate certain overseas GM bonds, and ended up selling the domestic bonds and buying the European equivalent. Sudi Mariappa, a specialist on that desk, said the firm captured "something on the order of 35 to 50 basis points" on the swap, owing mainly to the fact that GM bonds in Europe are less liquid than they are in the United States. A euro or yen investor could reach the same conclusion, or just take a view that European interest rates are less likely to rise than those of the United States, because its economic recovery is slower, or that the dollar will weaken further, and choose to withdraw (at least to some extent) from the American market. The immediate effect of this selling is reduced demand for U.S. Treasuries and lower prices.

All of these trends argue in favor of a more defensive fixed-income portfolio than that of five years ago, but not the need to build an ark. Just because investment returns do not come as easily in a bear market does not mean investors cannot thrive and prosper during one. Speaking of equity markets 80 years ago, Jesse Livermore could have been referring to the bond market today when he said: "Not even a world war can keep the stock market from being a bull market when conditions are bullish, or a bear market when conditions are bearish. And all man needs to know to make money is to appraise conditions." This is Bill Gross's forte. He says the inflation he foresees "is not so significantly higher that a bond investor should run entirely to cash or spend all their draft choices on defensive linemen. I think they need to still have a little focus on the wide receiver and the quarterback in terms of scoring some touchdowns. You're going to need some balance."

Gross recommends a six-prong approach to coping with the new bond-market environment. His goal is to deliver higher total returns than you can capture from a single bond investment without taking more risk than conditions warrant. He does not, for example, recommend high-yield corporate bonds because their yields have come down sharply in the last year. Yields are down because the market views junk bonds as less risky now than they were; defaults have ebbed from double digits in the recession and bear market to less than 6 percent now, and corporate balance sheets are building strength rather than drawing upon it. Gross views risk in relation to return; at $10\frac{1}{2}$ percent, he thought junk yields were too high, and was a buyer. At 8 percent he thinks they are too low; he has been a seller. Gross goes through the bond market like an intelligent shopper goes through the supermarket. Everything goes on sale.

Anti-Aging Formula

When interest rates are steadily falling, the risks of owning bonds of long duration diminish. The opposite is also true. Gross has contracted the duration of his portfolios from six years or even more to between four and five. (His portfolios have an intermediate duration by design.) In times of rising interest rates, bonds with higher durations face the possibility of greater price decreases than bonds with lower durations.

Shortening maturities means accepting lower yields. Especially for investors who rely on their bond portfolio to pay their bills, this is a hard reality to face, but a reality nonetheless. As interest rates rise, 20-year bonds will go down less than 30s; 10s will go down less still. A professional is forced to mark his bonds to market every day, and individual investors are not, but the lesson of Gross's approach to bond management is not to let capital lay fallow merely to pretend these lower values are a "paper loss." If you refused in 2000 to sell the Internet stocks you bought in 1999, you avoided a paper loss. But by 2001 it was far greater, and by 2002 greater still. Avoiding a paper loss stuck you with a far greater real loss. Bonds do not decline like Internet stocks, but they do decline. Short bonds will protect more of your capital than long ones in coming years. The higher coupons of the longer bonds will be erased by the capital losses.

The 10-year Treasury currently yields around 4.5 percent. In Gross's estimation this will not rise much above 5 percent in coming years, meaning risk to capital is much less than longer maturities. In a low-inflation world, that is sufficient not only to protect capital but to grow it. Five percent—and Gross sees that as the new regime in coming years, down from 6 percent in 1997, when he published his book—is an excellent foundation for a fixed-income portfolio when inflation is low. It is much more normal than bull-market rates of the last 20 years.

Interestingly, Gross is sticking to intermediate maturity bonds—and not abandoning everything for the lowest durations available. Why? He does not believe inflation is going to get all that high. Rates will go up, but not all that much, hence his preference for intermediate terms. (See Figure 8.1.)

Figure 8.1   U.S. Treasury Yields, 1994–2003

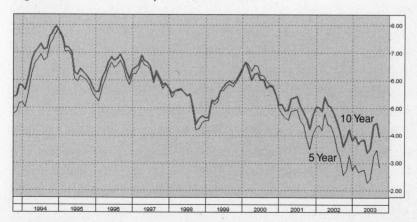

Source: PIMCO

Living on TIPS

John Brynjolfsson manages PIMCO Real Return Fund and is the firm's specialist on Treasury Inflation–Protected Securities, or TIPS. He says that when they were introduced six years ago, when inflation fears were almost nonexistent, they did not attract much attention and as a result were actually trading below par in the secondary market. The 10-year maturity, which currently guarantees a return of 2.25 percent plus the current rate of inflation, was trading at a real rate of 4 percent. Investors really began flocking to the issues in 2000, when the stock market began its dramatic decline, and their popularity has continued to increase, bringing their real returns to the guaranteed level. "The fall in inflation, the fall in equity market prices and the fall in bond yields is hammering home to baby boomers that their whole goal in retirement is to secure real returns on their current wealth portfolios," he says.

Gross regards TIPS as the single best idea for bonds in the coming five years. They are specifically designed for total return, rather than yield-oriented, investors. (In Canada they are called real return bonds.) Their guaranteed, or core, yield is all that is paid out in current income. The inflation adjustment is made to the bond's principal value, which increases in line with the non-seasonally adjusted U.S. City Average All Items Consumer Price Index for All Urban Consumers (CPI-U), a subseries of the broader index that does not favor rural residents over city dwellers. The index is published monthly by the Labor Department's Bureau of Labor Statistics. These increases accrue semiannually to the principal as the index rises; that is, the bonds' principal value grows. The first TIPS to be issued, which mature in 2007, have a total accrued value now of $1,160 for every $1,000 invested. In the unlikely event there is no inflation, or if deflation were actually to take the CPI down, the bonds mature at par. TIPS investors, therefore, are assured of receiving a total return that exceeds inflation; that is, which increases purchasing power, rather than merely protecting it.

TIPS do have a tax disadvantage, which is that imputed income, while being added to principal value and therefore not available to the shareholder, is nevertheless fully taxable in the current year. This is an annoyance that is familiar to mutual fund investors who reinvest dividends, as most do. Funds must distribute their gains to shareholders in order to avoid paying taxes on them themselves, and they typically do this in December. (Few equity funds will be making such distributions for years to come, having built up so many tax-loss carryforwards—the silver lining to the bear market cloud.) Even when distributions are reinvested, they are nevertheless taxable.

The painless way to avoid this burden is to own TIPS in a tax-deferred account, such as an IRA or 401(k), which indeed is the ideal home for all income-producing investments, aside from tax-free bonds. But as a practical matter this disadvantage is what two finance professors from Texas Tech University call "trivially different from that of conventional Treasury securities." Scott Hein and Jeffrey Mercer published a paper on the subject in 2003 and found that "TIPS generally have after-tax yields comparable to, if not exceeding, conventional securities."

Having paid taxes while owning the bonds, moreover, the increase to principal is not itself taxable when the bonds are redeemed. Investors are not stuck with a capital gain in addition to ordinary income because the imputed interest is the latter, not the former.

Investors in Brynjolfsson's fund, PIMCO Real Return, do receive income currently, because mutual funds never mature and therefore imputed income becomes real income as bonds are marked to their current market prices every business day.

Mortgaging the Future

Despite their peculiar vulnerability to interest rates, Gross and PIMCO are more committed to mortgage pass-through bonds than any other group. He recommended them in his book six years ago and recommended them again to me.

As explained in Chapter Five, mortgages have indeterminate durations; lower rates encourage homeowners to refinance, shortening them, and higher rates lead them to hold on, lengthening them—and both of these responses occur at the worst time for bondholders, who do not want their money back when rates are falling and do when they are going up. Therefore, they violate the principle of shortening duration as a defensive step in a bear bond market.

Mortgages also, however, have a structural feature that more than offsets this limitation, given Gross's view that interest rates will rise only modestly in coming years. "Homeowners are willing to pay an interest rate close to 2 percent higher than equivalent Treasury and agency notes," he says. "This 2 percent bonus is more than enough to compensate for the negatives of the options that the homeowner holds." In the 30 years that pass-throughs have been available—the first GNMA was issued in 1973—they have substantially outperformed their Treasury and agency counterparts. (See Figure 8.2.)

Mortgages are the biggest and most liquid domestic bond category, so they are the easiest bonds of all to buy. But they are also one of the

Figure 8.2   Mortgages versus Credits, 2002–2003

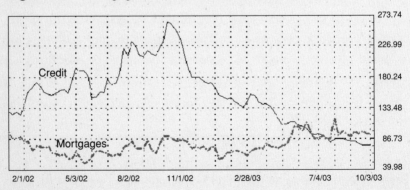

Source: PIMCO

most complex, because their prepayment features and other options change the risk structure of the underlying bond. PIMCO wrings extra performance out of them, with derivative strategies such as roll-downs that individual investors are not likely to be able to replicate successfully. Mutual funds are, therefore, a particularly efficient way to participate in the mortgage market.

Buying Your Local Brooklyn Bridge

As explained in Chapter Six, municipal bonds are particularly attractive now, and they appeal to Gross on a secular basis as well. "In bear markets municipals almost always perform very defensively," he says. "Their prices go down more slowly than do Treasuries and corporates."

State and local governments can perform very badly in hard times—witness California, whose rating has tettered on the edge of the junk heap. But this is rare. Many municipals are directly linked to regional infrastructure—such as toll roads, bridges, industrial parks, and sewer plants—that does not go away in recessions. General obligation bonds contain covenants requiring their issuers to take whatever steps are necessary—even tax increases—to assure that the bonds are fully serviced. "With the exception of California, these are damn good credits," Gross says.

Total return investors should be particularly interested in closed-end municipal bond funds—Gross owns most of his munis this way. They are discussed in Chapter Six. These funds are leveraged, and one thing to recognize is that the use of leverage in a bond portfolio increases its duration. That is, it does not mean the fund is buying longer bonds, but rather that the leverage increases the portfolio's interest-rate risk.

In its closed-end municipal funds, PIMCO uses leverage on a general ratio of one dollar of borrowed capital for every two dollars it receives from investors. PIMCO Municipal Income Fund, for example, has investor assets of $337.7 million and preferred, or borrowed, assets of $200 million; leverage accounts for 37 percent of the fund's total assets. The aim is to increase the portfolio's total return. PIMCO pays commercial-paper rates to borrow, currently in the range of 1 percent, and uses the money to buy bonds with average coupons in the 4.5 percent to 5 percent range—the same as Treasuries. (As explained in Chapter Six, muni yields are usually 15 percent or so less than Treasury yields, but currently they are nearly identical.) PIMCO Muni Income was yielding just over 7 percent at the time of writing, thanks to the coupons of those additional bonds. The fund pays a price, however, which is that the portfolio's duration extends correspondingly— in the case of this fund, to 9.67 years.

Also, closed-ends trade at market prices, rather than net asset value; PIMCO's muni closed-ends are all trading at premiums now, but a shift in investor sentiment that caused people to dump such funds could take their prices to discounts. So investors in closed-end funds must manage them as carefully as they would individual bonds. Although they invest in bonds, they trade like stocks. (See Figure 8.3.)

Figure 8.3   Share Price Chart of PIMCO Municipal Income since Inception

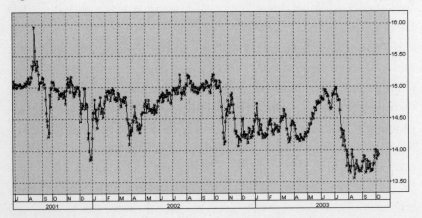

Source: PIMCO

Over There

With the Federal Reserve intent on reflating the domestic economy, the dollar is likely to remain under pressure compared with its foreign rivals, the euro and the yen. "An investor might want to protect against depreciation of the dollar, because that's what inflation leads to," Gross points out. This argues in favor of investing in the bonds of other developed countries, notably the German bund. This is a large and liquid market: The most actively traded futures contract in the world is listed in Frankfurt, on German bunds.

Aside from Japan, where interest rates approach zero, foreign government bonds provide attractive yields relative to their domestic competitor, the familiar Treasury. In the case of German bunds, they are yielding about 25 basis points less than corresponding Treasuries, owing to recent interest-rate reductions by the European Central Bank. Earlier in 2003, they were yielding as much as 50 basis points above Treasuries. Europe is experiencing downward pressure on interest rates because its economies are proving to be less resilient than our own, and are taking longer to recover from the global recession that began in 2001. Declining yields, however, signal rising bond prices, and Gross expects European government bonds to offer greater protection of principal than Treasuries in the years ahead. (See Figure 8.4.)

Add to this the currency play. If the dollar does not weaken, foreign bonds will return their yields and gains from lower rates. If it does, however, those returns will translate into more dollars for U.S. shareholders. A weakness in the greenback of 5 percent translates into a 5 percent gain on European bonds for dollar investors. Germany is not the only foreign government bond market in which Gross has been finding value. Great Britain's bonds are providing the highest real returns of any developed country in the world, and PIMCO has been a buyer.

Figure 8.4 German Bund and U.S. Treasury Yields, 1994–2003

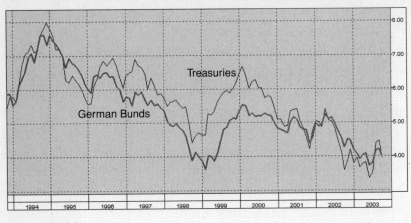

Source: PIMCO

As a matter of policy, PIMCO Total Return Fund hedges its investments in non–dollar-denominated bonds, meaning the fund itself is not making the move that Gross advocates for his personal portfolio and yours. Gross is generally averse to currency plays. In this case, however, he feels the secular argument is too strong to ignore for investors who can take advantage of it, even though his mutual fund cannot.

Figure 8.5 Euro versus Dollar since Its Inception

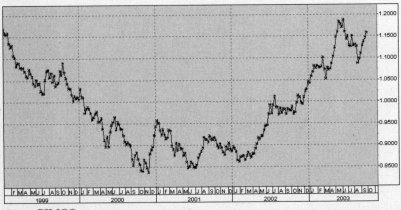

Source: PIMCO

Way Over There

Gross recommends "just a smidgeon" of high-quality emerging markets bonds. "Not a lot; just enough to juice up [a portfolio's] yield a little bit." The current environment is not one in which he is willing to accept much risk. Referring to the slogan of a brand of men's hair gel (before it was called gel), Brylcreem, he says, "It is an environment in which a little dab'll do ya."

A little dab of emerging markets debt has done wonders for fixed-income investors in recent years. PIMCO Emerging Markets Bond Fund, managed by Mohamed El-Erian, returned an annual average of 16.51 percent in the five years ended July 31, 2003. It was up 17.19 percent in the first seven months of 2003. It is the top-performing portfolio in its category, and indeed in all fixed-income categories, with the sole exception of a zero-coupon Treasury fund, American Century Target Maturity 2020. For reasons already explained in these pages, a long-term zero-coupon fund would be a very poor choice in the environment Bill Gross envisions for the five years to come.

Emerging markets endured a horrible period in the late 1990s, when economies from Thailand to Russia all but melted down. Some of them, notably Venezuela, continue to be condemned by local politics to be hostile to First World investors. But the fruits of globalism are tangible. One of the most striking examples is Brazil. Its current president is a former populist who, since taking office, has implemented policies to encourage foreign investment and property rights. Brazil's bonds at the depth of the Argentine-Venezuelan crisis traded at yields more than 1,500 basis points above U.S. Treasuries. That spread has since contracted to 640 points. Mexico and Russia have also compiled successful records that have attracted foreign investment. The increased flow of funds from the developed to the undeveloped world pushes up securities' prices in those markets all by itself, but it flows in only because of the prospect of real economic returns.

Like Gross, El-Erian distinguishes between "noise," which in developing markets are unsettled local politics, and fundamentals. The latter are rising in emerging countries, and in those nations where the noise is the cacophony of emerging democracy, as in Russia, it can reassure investors more than it worries them.

The debt of emerging nations, which is mostly the sovereign debt of its governments, although private bonds do trade, is a total return play because a large share of profits comes from capital gains. The average yields in the marketplace, about $8\frac{1}{2}$ percent, have accounted for only half the total returns.

Gross recommends that investors use professionally managed portfolios as their entry into emerging markets, because events there can impact bonds before most Americans even become aware of them. For example, Russia experienced a major five-day sell-off in its bonds recently, owing more to technical than fundamental reasons. El-Erian was bullish on Brazil early in the presidency of Luiz Inacio Lula da Silva when the developed world's press, such as Germany's *Deutsche Welle*, was proclaiming him a "leftist hero" who had invited Fidel Castro to his inauguration. The United States sent a minor trade delegate to the ceremony. Perhaps it should have sent El-Erian.

Weeding the Flowers

Five years from now, Gross expects that a portfolio constructed of these building blocks will have returned an annual average of 5 percent. "That's actually pretty good in a defensive battle," he notes. This is down markedly from an average of 8 percent over the last decade but, he says, "That's what happens to the bond market when you get this type of environment." Five percent is also within hailing distance of returns that many stock investors, such as Warren Buffett, expect. Historically, periods of securities' returns significantly higher than the norm are followed by periods of below-average results; finance professors call it reversion to the mean. The blowout 1990s have already led to one of history's most dramatic busts in the first decade of the twenty-first century.

Serious students of Gross's approach to investing will not be satisfied, however, with a garden of permanent plants. A bond portfolio is a living, dynamic garden that requires weeding and replanting. As surely as the bonds of Turkey or Poland or a Single-B rated American manufacturer appear unattractive now, they could become attractive under the right circumstances. The next chapter contains specific advice on how to plant, water, and weed your annuals and perennials—to create a bond garden like those of the pros.

CHAPTER 9

The Ways
of the King

By now, you understand the genius behind the Gross mystique. In a way unmatched by other legends of investing, Bill Gross is able to read the complex movements of the markets. It is almost as if he has senses the rest of us lack.

Like many great hedge fund managers and bond investors, Gross acts as an arbitrageur, able to see small but lucrative means of profit in the chaos of the markets and to pounce on mispricings with speed and fairly dependable accuracy. His eye is like Jesse Livermore's—only he has a Bloomberg, not a ticker tape machine—able to spot trends in the way bond prices move relative to the market and each other. A gambler as Ed Thorpe was, schooled by his weeks at the Four Queens, he has a card counter's technique that allows him to "read" the odds at any given moment. In his case, the odds are not whether an ace or face card is on top of the deck, but the bond-specific variables of inflation risk, duration, prepayment risk, and credit risk, and the ability to determine how they affect the attractiveness of individual bond prices. This

"micro" eye, the eye one sees in many of Wall Street's best, allows him
to trade with success.

This skill is not unique, although the level of Bill's ability is certainly
rare. Many great investors, Peter Lynch for example, have made millions spotting small errors in pricing and market timing—market inefficiencies, in other words—and these investors usually specialize in
the more inefficient sectors of the financial markets, areas like micro-
cap stocks, foreign stocks, and bonds and derivatives. Where Bill Gross
is unusual is that he is also able to see the markets with a soaring eagle's
macro eye, predicting major moves in interest rates, currencies, commodity prices, and inflation. His think tank of secular conference advisers certainly help his judgment, but this can hardly be discounted:
What leadership skill is more essential than the key presidential ability,
that of assembling the greatest team of advisors to help the one in the
predominant role?

Gross combines the microscopic trader's sense with the gut of a
Soros, a Buffett, and a Morgan. He has an uncanny—although imperfect—ability to spot trends in the broader economy, and to see how,
over the coming months and years, these trends will affect risks that
determine bond prices. He is able to strip emotion from the investing
process, to view the long-term horizon clearly like Baruch, even in periods of crashes and bubbles. This skill is not unique, either: It is the key
skill held by good fund managers. Where Bill is blessed is in his ability to combine the small, detailed instinct with a clear perception of the
big picture. He is able to use the information at his disposal to invest in
a manner that is very unlike Soros's: with very little risk, to achieve not
the crash of the Thai baht or fall of the British pound, but a solid,
workmanlike, dependable return, one that seems modest in any particular year, but that given Gross's consistency, is a virtual factory of
wealth production. This is what followers and admirers must emulate
should they wish to trade their bonds like Bill Gross.

There's a quick and easy way for you to take advantage of a tiny
bit of Bill Gross's brilliance: You simply have to buy shares in a

Gross-managed fund, like PIMCO's Total Return. Timid souls should take this route immediately and not read further.

The path for braver souls is not simple. By virtue of the tools available to one who invests such a large fund at an institution, Gross has a variety of instruments, notably the use of complex derivatives like swaps, at his disposal that you and I do not. So when it comes to replicating his investment approach in your personal portfolio, you will have to take somewhat more risk than he does to achieve the same result—50 to 100 basis points annually over the returns delivered by the Lehman Brothers Aggregate Bond Index.

The place to start is with a plan, which is divided into two parts—goals and the means of achieving them. The goal is easy: to beat the index (that is, the market) by 50 to 100 basis points. The means are many, but they come down to three basic decisions about sector allocation, duration, and opportunity. The first of these must be made through an analysis of the secular factors affecting the world economy. The second depends on your tolerance for risk. The last is based on relative values and will be the key driver in optimizing the returns of your portfolio.

Step One: Develop Your Own Secular Analysis

The first step in creating your own secular analysis is to recognize the information that you need to assemble. You do not need to have encyclopedic knowledge of world events or be on first name terms with world leaders. You do not have to experience the "rifle to the head" pressure of PIMCO's trading room to devote a little effort to keeping yourself apprised of the global economic scene and to reflecting on the investment implications of unfolding events. This does not imply hair-trigger trades when the *Wall Street Journal* flops onto your lawn or your desk each morning, but it does imply reading broadly and regularly. Restrict yourself to information you need to know, but cover it well.

The most important thing is that you keep abreast of the world's economies, following the media and business commentary on the shape of the U.S. economy, as well as those of the First World nations and the emerging markets. You should keep track of U.S. rates and read commentary anticipating how rates are going to move. In addition, you should familiarize yourself, to the extent you want to trade foreign bonds, with the interest rate environments, politics, and economies of nations overseas.

Gross is partial to *The Economist*, the British newsweekly that provides a comprehensive review of world affairs, political and social as well as financial. You can keep track of Lula and Jacques Chirac and industrial production in Australia, as well as Japan's wackiest new TV show and India's reigning heartthrob. It casts a European— but not *continental* European—eye on American affairs and fetches up more cosmopolitan articles than do domestic newsweeklies. *Barron's*, for example, while publishing unparalleled reams of economic and market data and making itself very valuable in the process, restricts itself to markets. If it were the only American periodical a foreign investor were to read, she would have a very incomplete view of Arnold Schwarzenegger and know even less about the Dixie Chicks. (The same thing might be said of a subscriber to the *New York Times*, for that matter.) *The Economist* grants itself a broader brief, regularly reporting on the social, political, and demographic trends that influence Gross's secular thinking. *The Economist* includes economic statistics as well as articles; one feature useful to international bond investors is its measurement of "purchasing power parity", also known as the "Big Mac" index. This chart states the price of a Big Mac (chosen because it is virtually identical wherever you buy one) around the world, converted into dollars; it is a useful guide to the relative value of currencies, although only an imperfect predictor of their eventual movements.

Knowledge of major demographic trends is hard to come by, as they are covered episodically by the major financial magazines and newspapers. As you follow the media, you should keep track of which industries are likely to prosper in the years ahead. Investing in their corporate bonds will reduce credit risk. You should also, given the size of the mortgage securities market, follow trends in U.S. real estate. Whenever particular companies or organizations assume a large percentage of your bond holdings, investigate them and understand what they do. Like Gross, you may discover a key flaw in an important company and break a story as important as his deconstruction of General Electric.

Gross also recommends reading books. He is a voracious reader himself. He believes investors should ground themselves in modern financial history to discern the patterns of human behavior they chronicle as well as the facts they record. An entire library of investment books without the word "Dummies" in them exists. People who have purchased *Reminiscences of a Stock Operator* from Amazon.com have also liked, the web site helpfully reports, *Extraordinary Popular Delusions and the Madness of Crowds* by Charles MacKay (Noonday Press, 1985), which documents all of the great financial scams, from tulip bulbs to the Ponzi scheme.

You can also learn a lot by creating, in your home area, a like-minded group of investors who can function as your very own secular forum. I suggest meeting monthly and asking each member to cover a particular area of the world economy each month. Ideally these topics should rotate throughout the group, so, for instance, you might cover real estate for one meeting, the euro-based economies the next, and trends in the U.S. economy the next. Specialization can allow you to research and read as much as possible about each of these important areas of knowledge, and, in the group you will benefit from the knowledge of others as well as through building your own.

For more detailed market information, Gross has recommended two sources, Bridgewater Associates and International Strategy & Investment Group (ISI). Bridgewater is a $42 billion institutional money manager that also publishes its research, including twice daily *Bridge-*

water Daily Observations. ISI is an investment advisory group whose economics chief, Ed Hyman, Gross highly regards.

PIMCO itself publishes considerable research and commentary, including Gross's own "Investment Outlook" column, McCulley's "Fed Focus", El-Erian's "Emerging Markets Watch" and Lee Thomas's "Global Markets Watch". The firm's web site, *www.pimco.com,* also stores general articles on bond investing, such as "Yield Curve Primer" and "Inflation Primer."

I would be remiss not to mention CNBC on MSN Money, for which I am a columnist. CNBC.com has been rated highly by both *Barron's* and *Forbes* in their annual reviews of online financial sites. The site is a venture between the MSN network and the financial television channel, where I appear weekly on the morning "Squawk Box" program.

The point of this research, of course, is to arm yourself with the information required to make intelligent three-month decisions about opportunities that arise in the fixed-income world, as well as to reaffirm your three-year views and over time to change them. If interest rates rise in coming years, as Gross expects, they could eventually choke off economic growth and engender rate cuts that would inaugurate a new bull market for bonds. A 7 percent yield on Treasuries might be the tipping point, the signal not only to buy them but to buy the longest of them. The inevitable recession will bring them down again, creating a bull market for Treasuries in which longer duration will become the brass ring, and junk bond yields will begin to sparkle, transforming them from pricey to dicey and thus creating opportunities for bargain-conscious shoppers.

Things do change. The sagacious and pithy Jesse Livermore reigned over markets that the Securities & Exchange Commission had yet to oversee; his heyday was over by the time modern securities laws were enacted. So one of his darkest observations has lost its bite. "The nature of the game as it is played is such that the public should realize that the truth cannot be told by the few who know," he told his Boswell in *Reminiscences.* Today, the truth can be difficult to unearth—

Gross was alone when he criticized General Electric's commercial paper—but a considerable industry is devoted to ferreting it out.

Step Two: Measure Your Risk Tolerance

The second step, assessing your personal risk tolerance, is an individual decision that requires some careful thought. To determine your personal tolerance, you must take into account your age and your dependence on your bond portfolio for income. Most investors allocate more funds to stocks when they are younger and less to bonds; the bond portion increases as you age and need more income from your investments, and is seen by most, correctly, as something of a safe haven. Thus, even if you have a high personal risk tolerance—let us say you are 30, retired from an internet company, with a wonderful golden parachute sitting in your brokerage account—you will not want to permit high risk in your bond portfolio. The decision is between low risk and even lower risk. The younger you are, and the less you need to access your capital or rely on the income, the more divergence you can allow from the index. You can, as I explain, allocate more to the flexible portion of your portfolio and less to the core.

Investors tend to focus on risk only when they consider investments that are "dangerous" or "risky"—plays on individual small-cap stocks, for example, or decisions to radically change asset allocation. This is a mistake. Risk is something to be considered when you look over your entire portfolio; what should really concern you is not the risk involved in each individual investment but the average risk of your entire portfolio. If you have 99 percent of your money invested in low-risk securities, it may seem like gambling to invest 1 percent in a high-risk bet on the markets. But it is not; your average risk is actually very low, and the decision should not be an emotional one. It should simply be a process of asking yourself: Is there a high enough possible return to justify taking a high-risk chance on 1 percent of the portfolio?

There are two ways to modify your bond holdings to reflect your personal tolerance for risk. One method would be to adjust the percentage of your bond holdings that you place in the flexible portfolio according to your age and income needs. In essence, this percentage equals the amount of risk you can accept, and the more risk you accept the more likely it is you will achieve Gross-like returns. Adopting this method is fairly easy. A younger person, aged 30 to 40, should consider reserving only 70 percent of their funds in the core portfolio; as you approach retirement age, this percentage should increase to 90 percent (for a retired person dependent upon bond income). However, this strategy causes a major problem: Only if you accept more risk in your bond portfolio can you truly adopt a Grossian strategy, for this requires you to make big bets when your educated gut tells you to do so

A second, better alternative is to place some of your nest egg, the money you need completely insulated from risk, in a separate account. This account would not be traded in a Total Return way. Two categories of bonds, tax-free municipals (munis) and Treasury Inflation–Protected Securities (TIPS), share characteristics that make them ideal for conservative investing. Because of the tax treatment of TIPS, they make an ideal investment for the portion of your tax-deferred account that requires risk-proofing. And, if you are in a high tax bracket, munis offer similar insulation in your personal, taxable accounts. Thus, for investors who are retired and need more secure money, an alternative is to keep the heavier traded, higher-risk, flexible portfolio at around 30 percent of your bond accounts, but to balance it by holding separate accounts for TIPS and munis that are outside your Total Return strategy. This does not mean you cannot invest in TIPS or munis in your Total Return fund—you should add them to the flexible portfolio if they present trading opportunities.

I recommend that older bond investors with higher income needs take this step, creating one or two "lockbox" accounts insulated from trading, if they are concerned about the level of risk implied in the

Gross strategy. Yet before you do this consider that, compared to most forms of investing, trading bonds in accordance with a Total Return strategy is fairly low-risk (unless you augment it with high-risk vehicles like zero-coupon bonds). You will not lose your nest egg. If your secular analysis turns out to be wrong, you will underperform against the benchmark but suffer little else. Only create these lockboxes if you absolutely, under no circumstances, can suffer a temporary loss of capital or income on a portion of your bond portfolio. If you have to have a certain amount of money to fund basic living expenses, fund that future obligation through TIPS and munis. If your financial setup is more flexible, you may not need to purchase this form of insurance, because it does come with cost: lower average returns than can be achieved through Total Return.

Once you have considered risk and decided what must be locked up and what can be made sensitive to some risk, you should dive into the main issue of this chapter: how to take advantage of relative values and the total return approach to win at the bond game.

Step Three: The Total Return Strategy

Implicit in the total return approach is the hypothesis that markets are dynamic and chronically subject to mispricing. You must convince yourself that at any moment virtually anything you own is subject to sale because *something else offers better relative value*, that is, the decision to sell a security implicitly relies on a decision to buy something better. This is an extreme value mindset, the opposite of market timing. Market timers think the whole marketplace can stink, and when it does they sell everything and go to cash. The total return approach relies on the assumption that an actively managed portfolio will beat the low returns delivered by cash in any market, short of global collapse. (If you are worried about the end of the world, buy shotgun shells and bottled water, not securities.) If you do not share in these assumptions, and many do not, the Gross method is not something you should adopt or have confidence in your ability to implement successfully.

Since the goal is to beat the index, the place to start building is with the components of the index itself. The Lehman Brothers Aggregate Bond Index, the most widely used benchmark for domestic bonds, is an amalgam of about 6,000 individual bonds in exact proportion to their weighting in the high-quality taxable bond marketplace. Three-quarters of them are rated Triple-A. About 35 percent of the index is weighted in mortgage-backed securities issued by Ginnie Mae, Freddie Mac, and Fannie Mae. Some 34 percent of the weighting goes to U.S. Treasuries and agencies. The credit sector, mainly corporations, accounts for 27 percent, with the balance distributed among trace amounts of foreign-government bonds and other securities. The average bond in the index has an intermediate duration of about four years. To be included, bond issues have to be substantial in size and to trade actively. The bonds represented by the index constitute a $7 trillion marketplace, a near doubling of its size only 10 years earlier.

An investor's core portfolio will be built, therefore, around mortgage, Treasury/agency, and corporate bonds. They will deliver more than 75 percent of the portfolio's total return each year, so their selection requires careful attention. But the balance of the portfolio will provide the extra juice that takes total portfolio returns above the benchmark, so managing this supplemental or flexible mix of securities is the heart of the total return approach.

It is tempting to relate words like "core" and "flexible" to "secular" and "cyclical" as we have used them in these pages—assuming that the core portfolio reacts to secular changes and the flexible to cyclical—but doing so would be a mistake. Secular refers to trends that take years to unfold, and cyclical to changes within shorter periods of time; however, both the core and the flexible components of the portfolio are built on a secular foundation and adjusted in response to cyclical conditions. For example, mortgage bonds are always a central element of the portfolio (because a secular analysis right now is positive for mortgage bonds), but you will own fewer of them sometimes and more of them at other times (in response to cyclical trends and events).

PIMCO was a huge seller of mortgage bonds in the summer of 2003, and when I was interviewing Gross for his key investment ideas he was reluctant to mention mortgages because they had been battered so badly when long-term interest rates spiked from little more than 3 percent to 4.5 percent. "Sometimes I don't mention them because I'm more enthusiastic about TIPS and municipals and emerging markets," he told me. "I tend to forget that since mortgages almost always dominate PIMCO portfolios, we should talk about them, too." A key element of your added value must be not just in the selection and trading of bonds in the flexible part of the portfolio, but in your decision to adjust the percentages held in the mortgage-backed, Treasuries, and corporate sectors of the core portfolio. Like Gross, you may decide that mortgage-backs are going to undergo a rough few months; as a result, you may shade your allocation to them from 30 percent (if that is the allocation within the Lehman index at that time) to 25 percent or even 20 percent. You will still maintain a core holding in mortgage-backed securities. However, you will shadow the index in a way that mirrors its nature but diverges from the strict percentage allocations of its sectors, occasionally taking big bets.

This skill is similar to that employed by active equity managers who run large-cap funds. Because of the constant pressure to beat the index, their holdings at any moment are a slightly different, personalized version of the appropriate index. If the stocks of two companies within the index are so highly correlated that there is virtually no alpha[1] to be gained from owning both, they pick whichever they think has the brightest prospects. If these equity managers are privy to the belief that the construction or telecommunications sector is about to experience a crisis, or if they understand a particular holding to be

---

[1]Or, return relative to the risk involved compared to the index's predicted return.

troubled, they do not sell all—they pare down the holding relative to the index. If they have had a good year and can take more risk, they might add to their holdings of stocks with higher standard deviations relative to the index, betting that conditions will be right for their prices to improve, and thus that they will outperform the market.

Shadowing the index always involves the assessment and management of risk; in our portfolio, this is handled through the precise measurement and allocation given to sector weightings and duration. It was the risk of radically lengthening durations that sent mortgages into the doghouse. An upward spike in mortgage rates will always choke off refinancings, meaning notes that would have been refinanced in only months (that is, very short duration) may now be held for years (intermediate or even long duration). Our risk tool, therefore, is double-edged. One side of the blade allows us to differ from the index in our allocation in a way that might allow us to take security risk, increasing our emerging markets holdings—if we believe that it is a good decision to make. But the other blade edge is equally important; it slices and dices the mix of short, intermediate, and long maturities, allowing us to differentiate our portfolio from the durations held by the index to our advantage.

To say the same thing another way, there are times, such as now, when Treasury bonds are not the least risky securities in the marketplace but the most. Long Treasury bonds have the greatest interest rate risk of all bonds. From the point of view of designing our portfolio, therefore, long Treasuries are a flexible holding that will usually be absent, except in times of falling rates. The portfolio's core is built around intermediate-term notes. Indeed, all of the core holdings will be intermediate term. Duration adjustment will occur around the portfolio's fringe. The next time your secular forecast assumes gradually and consistently declining interest rates for three or more years, your flexible holdings will bulk up on long maturities, including the longest Treasuries you can find. This is not Gross's secular forecast now, however, so let other people buy the 30-year Treasuries you are selling. In a regime of rising interest rates, they will languish.

Your portfolio building blocks will vary with your budget. If you have the half-million dollars Gross believes is the minimum necessary to hold down commissions, and you have confidence in your ability to purchase individual securities, then you should do so. You will be dealing almost always in the highest-quality, most-liquid bonds so your commissions (which are built into a bond's price, rather than explicitly priced) will be low. When you venture into more exotic markets, like junk or emerging markets, even you will use mutual or closed-end funds, as Gross does. If your budget is more modest, you can use funds for all your building blocks. Your aim is always to have the best possible management of your money.

Assuming you agree with the Gross approach and want to create a portfolio that shadows the Lehman Aggregate but outperforms in your core holdings, you will always hold its prime constituents, which are mortgages, Treasuries, and corporates. One easy way to do this, if you are a fund investor, is to dedicate a certain, floating percentage of your bonds to an index fund, like the Vanguard Total Bond Market Index Fund. This fund follows the index fairly faithfully, lagging over the five years ended August 31, 2003, by 39 basis points a year, which reflects its expense ratio of 10 basis points and such other costs as trading commissions. Indices themselves do not have such expenses, which is why index funds cannot beat them. If you can buy individual securities, you can replicate the index exactly in your core holding, and, while you will have expenses, too, they do not include the expense ratio, which goes to pay the manager. If your portfolio is sufficiently large, therefore, you can replicate the index in the core yourself and keep those 10 basis points. This means you are already 10 percent to 20 percent closer to meeting your goal. It also means you are responsible for security selection, of course, and that is beyond the scope of this book. Bill Gross is a "big picture" guy and, besides, there are 6,000 individual bonds in the index, of which you will own only a few. Your time spent copying the activity of the index is an additional cost that may not be worth 10 basis points to you. But, assuming it is, you must faithfully copy the movements of the index in your core portfolio by a regular program of trading.

In the core, you can safely disregard the trace constituents of the index and focus on mortgages, Treasuries, and corporates. The core will constitute 75 percent of your portfolio and be relatively unchanging. The weighting in the index does change over time; 30 years ago mortgage pass-throughs barely existed, and 20 years from now some hitherto unknown security may become important. The core will play keep-up with these trends but on a secular basis; it will not be reweighted more often than once a year, and usually less. Currently it is allocated along these lines:

- 37 percent in mortgage pass-throughs, which in turn will be a mix of Fannies, Freddies and Ginnies, in a ratio of three Fannies to two Freddies to one Ginnie Mae.
- 35 percent in Treasuries and agencies, in a ratio of two Treasuries to one agency.
- 28 percent in corporates, at least three-quarters of them rated Triple-A. These will be broadly diversified by sector, such as autos and pharmaceuticals.

The duration of the core will be four years, in accord with the index itself. Managing duration will be done in the flexible portfolio, but much of the duration that has to be managed is affected by swings in the index. In the summer of 2003, the duration of mortgage pass-throughs tripled as rates rose. Since they are the largest component of the core, lengthening its duration involuntarily, active steps would have been required in the flexible portfolio to bring down this significant new risk.

The flexible portfolio, which accounts for 25 percent of your fixed-income assets, therefore will frequently contain bonds suitable for the core, including mortgages. That is, your personal exposure to mortgages can be greater or less than that of the index, regardless of the fact that you always own plenty of them. The secular outlook for mortgages is very compelling, regardless of whether interest rates are high or low; they offer more carry than Treasuries. In a regime of stable interest rates, a significant portion of the flexible portfolio will be invested in mortgages. When rates are rising, you could own none in the flexible portfolio. They are added and subtracted to the mix primarily to adjust your duration risk, accepting more of it when rates are falling and scaling back as they rise. This portion of the flexible portfolio is the portion you should use to add or subtract to your overall allocation (versus the index), based on your secular outlook for the future.

It is, fortunately, considerably easier to create in your core and flexible portfolios a shadow bond index than it would be if you were to create a shadow equity index. In an equity portfolio, you have to worry more about individual securities. As credit risk in the main sectors is so low, you simply do not, as a practical matter, have to worry much about individual issues. The analysis is only a sector analysis. This is because of the credit advantages given to bondholders: Even in the event of bankruptcy, you have a good chance of recovering your money. You should only worry if certain companies become large portions of your portfolio, when, like Bill Gross, you may need to decide if G.E.'s paper is risky or safe.

If you were managing stocks, the situation is very different. There you have to worry about a secular analysis—if consumer cyclicals will outperform consumer durables, for example—and an individual security analysis. Shadow index equity managers can make considerable returns by substituting stocks in ways that diverge from the index. They might sell Exxon-Mobil and substitute a different energy company; they might drop their holding in Merck & Co. and buy Pfizer, based on an individual analysis of the stocks. They have to consider on a daily basis if UPS or FedEx is the better shipping company to own. In the bond universe, this analysis should take up very little of your time, only to be considered if there is serious reason to become concerned about the credit risks of any of the corporate holdings in the core and flexible portfolios. If you hold the core and this portion of the flexible portfolio in funds, this worry is nonexistent.

The flexible portfolio will also contain all of your exposure to the more volatile fixed-income classes, notably high-quality foreign-government bonds, emerging markets debt and domestic high-yield (junk) bonds. This is the opportunistic portion of your holdings, in which you are looking for the greatest likelihood of superior yields, capital gains, or both. Regardless of the size of your portfolio, you will almost certainly choose to own these assets in the form of funds, whether mutual or closed-end. Once again index funds are an option but, since you are not a long-term investor in these areas and are picking them instead because you think the wind will be at their back, active management is superior. Some actively managed funds will always beat their indexes and, since you are not a long-term shareholder, you can take advantage of their "hot hands" (their momentum) without fear that in a few years things will cool. In a few years you do not have to be there; even if your secular outlook compels you to remain in that marketplace, it does not require you to stick with that manager. Assuming this portion of the flexible portfolio is invested in funds, you must concern yourself not with credit risk or currency risk, but with manager selection.

The mix of sectors and securities in the flexible portfolio will change frequently, at least quarterly, and even more often when circumstances arise that require a change, such as a move in interest rates or significant geopolitical shifts in politics or policy. Sometimes, like Gross, you must be prepared to take big bets within the flexible portfolio. The model portfolios I suggest below, therefore, are necessarily general, and must be tweaked for optimal performance. They do, however, suggest the themes Bill Gross has identified as having the most impact on total returns, notably carry and duration. Each of them is designed to deliver 50 to 100 basis points more than the Lehman Aggregate in the climate each describes. All short-term adjustments to the portfolio are made in this flexible element of the portfolio.

However, some opportunistic investments do not conveniently fall into the categories available to investors in funds. The sovereign debt of developed nations, for example, can be attractive to U.S. investors because rates there are high when ours are low, or because the dollar is weakening. The opposite can be true, due to cross-currents in the geopolitical climate rather than more general conditions. Right now Gross recommends such bonds for reasons explained in Chapter Eight. But these bonds are not accounted for in the model portfolios because these conditions do not lend themselves to categorization. To take full advantage of your portfolio you have to be willing to gamble—Gross does not disapprove of this word, even if J.P. Morgan did—on the transitory and unpredicted. Openness to opportunity is the hallmark of total return investing. Trim back your other flexible holdings to make room for the unexpected.

TIPS do not easily fit into the categories established for bonds, first because they are a relatively new security, and second, because their nature allows you to use them in two ways. Given the high carry of TIPS (at the moment), an excellent case can be made for their inclusion in a relatively high proportion in the flexible portfolio. But, since TIPS are structured as "real return bonds," they also belong in the second core portfolio I discussed above, the one designed to provide rainy day money. By varying the durations of the TIPS you hold to respond to the movements in the yield curve, you can trade them to avoid the losses that holders of all types of Treasuries face in a rising curve—the situation we have as this book went to press (October 2003). They offer you a "lockbox" for money you absolutely must have to fund existing future obligations, such as mortgage payments or other forms of debt. They also offer you a way to reduce your personal risk, if that is your desire. Readers who are close to retirement age should consider holding some funds in TIPS outside of their Gross portfolio as the ultimate safe haven for necessary money. Younger readers with fixed obligations due in the future may want to use TIPS to invest college savings or other obligations.

There is a potential risk with TIPS that experts debate at the moment—the securities are so new in the United States that many questions about them are unanswered. The issue concerns the Consumer Price Index (CPI), used of course to measure the bonus payments that TIPS make as they reach maturity. There is a strong debate among economists right now concerning the CPI: many believe it overvalues inflation. Facing a huge deficit, the federal government has a vested interest in restructuring the way the CPI is calculated to reduce the monthly figure. This would, first of all, look good to the voters—but it would also reduce the government's future obligation on TIPS (and reduce guaranteed wage and contract price increases, often linked in contracts directly to the CPI). If policymakers manage to wrangle with the math used to calculate the CPI (itself based on the price changes of a basket of goods chosen in a somewhat arbitrary manner), TIPS will suddenly produce less of a bonus and, if Washington took this to extremes, they could actually end up underestimating inflation and not providing a real return. This risk is one reason, apart from illiquidity, why TIPS have a higher carry. Although the current carry makes TIPS somewhat attractive, buying them is in a sense placing a bet that the CPI is not overhauled by the government. TIPS are also appropriate in any economic environment if you want to gamble that inflation will actually exceed the consensus prediction. If you want to make those bets, buy them—otherwise, since they are insulated from the working of the yield curve, we will consider them as appropriate for a nest egg fund but not for the standard flexible portfolio (and not for the core portfolio, either, as they are not constituents of the Lehman index).

Whether you adjust the core-flexible balance to account for age and income needs or keep a side fund invested 100 percent in TIPS, you should adjust the holdings in both core and flexible portfolios to take into account current economic conditions.

When Conditions Are Stable

Bonds are affected more by changes in interest rates than their absolute level; in stable conditions, therefore, bond prices do not move very much. The yield curve is considered "normal", gently sloping upwards, in these unusual, calm periods, where inflation and interest rates are assumed to be stable for the future but longer-term investors are slightly more rewarded than shorter-term investors (because of the inherent risks of lending money to an enterprise for a longer period).

A regime of political and economic calm rewards investors who accept modest sector and duration risk. In a strong economy, corporate bonds are well supported and the flexible portfolio should contain corporates to increase the allocation versus the index. In foreign markets risks are also lower, and the carry offered by emerging markets debt is attractive—thus, the flexible portfolio should contain a higher number of emerging-market bonds than normal. Holdings in developed country debt, especially of the largest economies, should also be increased. Note, however, that stable conditions can exist in the United States and not overseas; adjustments to the holdings in foreign government debt and emerging-market bonds should be made to reflect this.

Stable yield curves often presage times of economic growth. In late 1984, just before the start of the Reagan boom, the curve was stable; in the ensuing years, until the Gulf War, the economy rose like a phoenix. It was a particularly good time to own junk bonds. Stable curves are actually considered a "buy" signal for high-yield, likely to perform well in the next months as good conditions encourage creditors not to worry about risk; few liquidations and bankruptcies occur.

Core and opportunistic investment alternatives are both attractive in stable times. This is a time for balance and for just a few big bets—the potential play on high-yield and emerging markets paper.

The flexible portion of the portfolio will be aligned like this (see Figure 9.1):

- 15 percent in long Treasuries
- 15 percent in mortgages
- 15 percent in long high-quality corporates
- 15 percent in junk bonds
- 15 percent in First World foreign sovereign debt
- 15 percent in emerging markets debt
- 10 percent in TIPS

Figure 9.1   When Conditions Are Stable

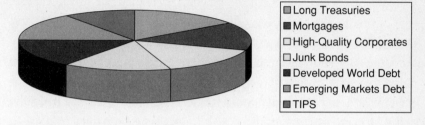

- ◻ Long Treasuries
- ◼ Mortgages
- ◻ High-Quality Corporates
- ◻ Junk Bonds
- ◼ Developed World Debt
- ▨ Emerging Markets Debt
- ◼ TIPS

When Interest Rates Are Rising

This is the regime that confronts us as this book goes to press. The yield curve is rising more sharply than before, indicating investors' assumption that times will get better, growth will improve and inflation will rise along with it. Inflation risk is increasing, making mortgages particularly unattractive, owing to their indeterminate duration. They should be eliminated entirely from the flexible portfolio, though not from the core. Long Treasuries are anathema; they are hurt the worst in an environment of rising rates.

Rising rates also imply higher borrowing costs from corporations, and especially junk bond issuers; opportunities for capital gains are disappearing and risks to their coupons are increasing. It is not a fatal environment for them, but a dangerous one. Sophisticated investors use the rising curve as a signal to sharply reduce their high-yield debt holdings. They get out before the inevitable crash comes.

By the same token, rates rise when the economy is strengthening, which is a positive sign for emerging markets that are heavily reliant on U.S.-related trade. Emerging markets bonds often show great appreciation (along with their perpetually high yields) during these periods; so long as you sell them before recession looms, you should maintain or increase their presence in the flexible portfolio.

In the current environment, the rising curve coincides with a favorable time for investment-grade foreign bonds—but this is due to the weakness of the dollar. Although U.S. interest rates are projected to increase (an event that normally makes currencies rise in value), foreign investors are dumping dollars, pushing the currency down and raising the value of foreign investments. In creating your flexible portfolio, the allocation given to foreign investments must be heavily influenced by your projection of the dollar's future versus other major currencies. Under normal conditions, a rising curve signals a bad time to hold foreign investments because it is usually accompanied by a rise in the dollar. Thus, in this model, First World foreign bonds are absent, because the current conditions are unusual and this is a general guide.

The current environment has a rising curve but it is not rising too steeply (as it does in an inflation panic). This environment is perfect for bonds of intermediate maturities. In a craze or a wild boom—the exception is the 1990s boom, when stocks exploded, everyone earned Monopoly® money, but inflation was low—the yield curve rises very sharply, and then you want to be holding short-term bonds. When things revert to normal, they will have the highest appreciation of the bunch. (See Figure 9.2.)

When rates are rising, the best kind of Treasuries to own are TIPS. Rising rates are a symptom of accelerating inflation, or at least the fear of greater inflation, against which these securities protect.

- 40 percent in short-term Treasuries (1–3 years)
- 40 percent in intermediate TIPS (3–7 years)

Figure 9.2   When Rates Are Rising

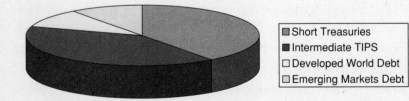

- 0 percent in mortgages
- 10 percent in First World foreign sovereign debt
- 10 percent in emerging markets debt

When Interest Rates Are Declining

This is the happiest time for fixed-income investors; the 20-year bull market in bonds from the early 1980s through the early 2000s represented what Gross has called bond investors' salad days. Duration risk diminishes greatly for long Treasury bonds, and their role in the portfolio can become very significant. It also declines for mortgages. Credit risk increases, however, because lower rates usually imply a softening economy or even recession. Corporate bonds will suffer, and junk bonds are poison because defaults will rise. In a stable economy, the default rate on junk bonds can be as low as 2 percent; in the early years of the twenty-first century it soared above 10 percent. Similarly, emerging nations will be facing a slowdown in their markets. So the flexible portfolio will happily sacrifice the carry offered by credits in favor of the lush gains on offer from the highest-quality bonds.

Judging when interest rates are going to decline significantly is, of course, very difficult, but the yield curve on Treasuries offers some clues. It is, in effect, a consensus of the future, a mechanism through which investors reveal their collective predictions for interest rates across maturities. In times when there *may* be a recession, the yield curve signals this by becoming flat or humped. Unfortunately, this is not a perfect signal: Sometimes the curve reverts to normal or rising without a recession happening in between.

An intriguing example happened in April 1989, when the yield curve developed a hump (the highest rates were for medium-term bonds, not the shortest or the longest). This predicted the recession of the early nineties with stunning accuracy. Certainly a humped curve is a major warning signal: It signals rough times ahead for high-yield and emerging market bonds and a flight to quality. It can be a good time to buy long-term high-quality debt and to sell junk and emerging markets. If you bet on bad times, you will make out well—if it was a blip on the horizon, nothing more, you will lose a substantial portion of the return you could have made.

When the economy falls directly into recession, the yield curve can become inverted. Investors expect rates to fall in the future and expect lower yields on longer-term debt. By the time this pattern appears it is usually too late to get out of high-yield and risky bonds in time—the flight to quality will already have happened.

A period of falling rates is, for those who want to inject more risk into their bond portfolios, the one time to buy zero-coupon bonds. Zero-coupons of long duration are the riskiest investments a bond investor can hold: They are very similar to bets placed at the roulette table. If you are convinced beyond doubt that rates will fall, they can add significant value. If rates rise, however, you will lose your shirt. Shorter-duration zeros add less risk and are more palatable for most investors, but, again, they are only successful in times of falling rates and must be sold before rates rise again.

In times of inverted curves, or true recessions, your flexible portfolio should include bonds of the highest quality. If your secular analysis persuades you that the other important countries will also reduce rates, this can be a good time to hold high-quality foreign sovereign debt. As reduced rates usually signal a fall in the dollar, these times are usually excellent times to own foreign sovereign debt. If you are an optimist, or at least someone able like Bernard Baruch to ignore the hubbub when everyone around you is talking about a crash, then load up on bonds of long durations. When the market comes back and the curve reverts to normal, Treasuries with the longest maturities bounce back the most.

I recommend the following (see Figure 9.3):

- 35 percent in long Treasuries (10 years and up)
- 30 percent in mortgages

- 20 percent in long TIPS
- 10 percent in intermediate-term corporates
- 5 percent in First World sovereign debt

I have left convertible bonds (converts) out of these model portfolios, because they function quite differently from regular bonds. The equity component of a convert makes it sensitive to movements and pricing on the stock market, a risk absent from every other class of bond—except when a stock swoons to a degree that causes bondholders to worry about credit risk. Total Return investors should stay away from converts unless they plan to become experts in the stock market as well; if you are able to judge the fairness of a convert's valuation (just like assessing the value of an option to buy stock at a set price in the future) then go ahead, trade in this market. If you are not a stocks expert, stay away.

Although these models address the flexible portfolio, by their nature they are based on secular analysis. No one can foresee the exact circumstances that will occur during each of these three archetypal periods. Gross-style investing requires that the investor be willing and able to respond to unique circumstances, and they are sometimes inexplicable. 1998, the year of the Russian default, was a bleak disaster for the bonds of developing nations, and it had little to do with movements in or predictions for future movements in U.S. rates, which happened to be declining at the time. But generally these models reflect

Figure 9.3   When Rates Are Falling

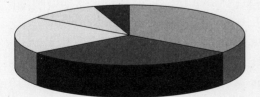

what has actually happened to these assets under the conditions described. Junk bonds had their best year in the last 10 in 1993, when rates were stable, and did miserably both before, during, and immediately after the recession of 2001. They have just been through an extremely sunny period; with the curve rising more sharply, now is the time to get out.

A true Grossian investor should consider the yield curves in Great Britain, Germany, and other large markets, as well as each country's unique political factors, before deciding on whether or not to buy or sell their sovereign debt. The general principle, which the past decade has completely violated, is that expectations of rising rates suggest a higher dollar and falling rates a lower dollar. However, the dollar's value is influenced by so many political factors this can sometimes not be the case. Many Asian countries, including China, buy and sell dollars on the currency markets in huge amounts to artificially keep their currencies low and promote exports. This mechanism worked in the past decade to keep the dollar artificially high, as the Asian countries continually bought dollars despite falling rates, and sold their own currencies, to reduce demand and hence the value of the yuan and yen. Recent doubts about the United States' future as an economic superpower and the vogue for the euro have forced the dollar down, even though the markets (in the yield curve) expect rates to go up over the next few years. The European stability pact has forced the major European markets to keep rates higher than they are here; as a result, their yield curves are rising less sharply than ours. While all of these factors have to be addressed by investors, the standard rule is to bulk up on highly rated sovereign debt when the dollar is trending downwards (usually when the curve is falling) and to sell when it is appreciating (when rates are rising or expected to rise).

Investing the Gross way implies taking risks and occasionally making big bets. This must be rooted in a careful analysis of the markets with as much emotion removed as possible. With Mr. Spock-like stoicism, you must consider the future for interest rates, for real estate, currencies, and international economies. When you see an opportunity, pounce on it by betting up to 5 percent of your flexible portfolio on the outcome—and as your account appreciates, consider raising your stakes.

You can also increase your risk and your potential return by using leverage, the leverage available when you buy shares in closed-end funds. Naturally, the fund you select should reflect in its holdings your analysis of the economy and the yield curve, and therefore the appropriate mix of bonds and the appropriate duration.

Two techniques you should consider for managing duration are the "bullet" and the "barbell." These are used at times when intermediate-term bonds offer the best potential returns, usually when the curve is stable or rising gently. Gross currently believes that the U.S. economy faces strong challenges in the future and that we will not see a major growth period like the 1990s again for some time; as a result, he believes that while rates may rise for a while they will not rise very much for the next five years. He is therefore assuming a normal or slightly rising curve, and therefore he is concentrating on intermediate-term bonds.

There are two ways to ensure that your portfolio's average duration is similar to that enjoyed by intermediate-term bonds: Buy intermediate-term obligations or buy short-term and long-term bonds in equal measure, so the two average each other out. The first method, the bullet, is used when the curve is not in danger of humping. If, however, Gross were predicting a period of a humped curve, the usual precursor to a recession, he would use the opposite approach, the barbell. When the curve is humped, rates are highest and prices lowest for intermediate-term bonds, and it is better to have had your money in the two other sectors. If, like Gross, you predict a period of slow growth or little growth, stick to the bullet and purchase intermediate-term issues of Treasuries and corporates (this can be done in both core and flexible portfolios). If your analysis predicts a recession, or at the least, a major recessionary scare, adopt the opposite barbell approach.

The choice of technique offers another way to "beat" the index even in the core portfolio without adding risk, as the average duration of your bonds is equal with either approach.

For fund investors, without the minimums necessary for separate accounts, PIMCO operates mutual funds in all of these categories, and closed-end funds in most of them. Your choices are featured in Table 9.1.

If you were to use PIMCO funds to implement these model portfolios, here is how they would fit. Bear in mind that these funds are used in the flexible portion of your portfolio, and are not long-term holdings. For the core, the mutual fund choice is either the diversified general bond fund managed by Bill Gross, PIMCO Total Return, or an index-tracking Vanguard fund. Due to PIMCO's long history with two investment companies that evolved out of client relationships, Gross also manages two no-load funds, Fremont Bond Fund and Harbor Bond Fund.

Long Treasuries   PIMCO Long-Term U.S. Government Fund has a duration of 10.8 years, and can be used to extend the portfolio's duration.

Low Duration   PIMCO Short-Term Fund has a duration of 0.9 years, which puts it into the near-cash category. In contrast, PIMCO Low Duration has a duration of 2.4 years, which makes it a true bond fund, as opposed to a near-cash fund. The Short-Term fund, therefore can be used to reduce your overall portfolio's duration sharply; the Low Duration fund is used to shrink duration more modestly.

Mortgages   The closed-end PIMCO Commercial Mortgage Trust differs from its siblings in that it owns business, rather than residential, mortgages. As such, it is more subject to the business cycle than the home building and refinancing industries; a real estate rather than a conventional mortgage fund. It does not fit quite as neatly into the mortgage pigeon hole in our flexible portfolio, except for this: Closed-

Table 9.1 PIMCO Mutual Fund Choices

Investment Category	Fund (Ticker)	Mutual (M) or Closed-End (C)
Convertibles	PIMCO Convertible Institutional (PFCIX)	M
Corporate, high yield	PIMCO High-Yield Institutional (PHIYX)	M
	PIMCO High Income Fund (PHK)	C
	PIMCO Corporate Opportunity Fund (PTY)	C
Corporate, high quality		
Intermediate	PIMCO Investment Grade Corporate Institutional (PIGIX)	M
	PIMCO Corporate Income Fund (PCN)	C
Emerging markets	PIMCO Emerging Markets Bond Institutional (PEBIX)	M
Floating rate	PIMCO Floating Rate Income Fund (PFL)	C
Foreign bond	PIMCO Foreign Bond Institutional (PFORX)	M
General bond	PIMCO Total Return Institutional (PTTRX)	M
Low duration	PIMCO Short-Term Institutional (PTSHX)	M
	PIMCO Low Duration Institutional (PTLDX)	M
Mortgages		
	PIMCO GNMA Institutional (PDMIX)	M
	PIMCO Total Return Mortgage Institutional (PTRIX)	M
	PIMCO Commercial Mortgage Trust (PCM)	C
U.S. Government		
Long	PIMCO Long-Term U.S. Government Institutional (PGOVX)	M
TIPS	PIMCO Real Return Institutional (PRRIX)	M
World bond	PIMCO Global Bond Institutional (PIGLX)	M
	PIMCO Strategic Global Government Fund (RCS)	C

end funds are usually more like economical trading vehicles than mutual funds, which can have sales and redemption charges. Since the flexible portfolio is a trading portfolio, therefore, this fund can be the best choice. If you can purchase the mutual funds PIMCO GNMA and PIMCO Total Return Mortgage economically, such as the institutional shares in a retirement or wrap account, however, they are more suitable.

These differ from each other in that GNMAs are backed by the full faith and credit of the U.S. government, and other mortgage bonds are not. By prospectus, PIMCO GNMA holds at least 80 percent of its assets in Ginnie Maes. PIMCO Total Return Mortgage has a majority of assets in higher-yielding Fannies and Freddies. So the GNMA fund is the more conservative of the two funds.

High quality corporates   PIMCO Corporate Income Fund

Junk bonds   PIMCO High Income Fund

Emerging markets   PIMCO Emerging Markets Bond

The above portfolios are designed without regard for taxes. Investors in the middle and lower brackets, and in qualified retirement plans like IRAs and 401(k)s, can expect them to deliver greater total returns than tax-free alternatives. But investors in the top income tax brackets can frequently do best by focusing the high-quality portion of their portfolio on municipal bonds and bond funds. Certainly the current environment, in which municipals are delivering the same returns as Treasuries, favors tax-free bonds even in lower brackets. This unusual situation is not expected to persist. However, if your analysis persuades you that it will (and this will be the case if states continue to face severe fiscal crunches and higher credit risk) you should then, and only then, buy tax-frees even if the tax advantages are irrelevant to you. They become, as they have in the past few years for Gross, a pure carry play, a trading opportunity. For investors convinced of this outside the highest tax brackets, closed-end municipal funds should be monitored and purchased when they are advantageous and sold when this advantage disappears. These high-quality securities substitute for domestic high-quality bonds such as corporates and mortgages in the flexible portfolio.

High-bracket investors face a different choice, because for them municipals are both a core and a flexible option. In some circumstances, the entire core portfolio can be devoted to them as well as, more opportunistically, part of the flexible portion. Munis can also be used to create a second nest egg portfolio for taxable investors who need to keep a rainy day fund for investments outside their tax-deferred accounts. If you are in this situation, you should consult your tax adviser as part of planning your total portfolio.

I should stress that these are my own ideas, developed over a career of financial journalism, and not the official recommendations of PIMCO. The company is not in the financial advice business, although its distribution arm, PIMCO Funds, works through brokers and financial advisers. PIMCO Funds was not consulted in the preparation of these recommendations.

The active, total return investor takes satisfaction, and even pleasure, from one-upping Wall Street through skill, hard work, and careful attention to events, moderated by an overriding vision of one's goals and the means of achieving them. I hope that I have given you some tools for developing a fixed-income portfolio that delivers superior returns with very modest risk. The market's usual cacophony relegates bonds to a bleak and uninteresting safe harbor. In fact it is a vaster world than equities comprise, and none of its players has shown greater skill in exploring and exploiting it than Bill Gross. The rewards are great. Now that you know some of his tricks, apply them to your own portfolio and watch it grow.

Sources

Unless otherwise noted, all interviews were conducted with employees of Pacific Investment Management Company, both in person at the company's Newport Beach, California, headquarters and on the phone.

Introduction

Between February and October 2003, the author conducted interviews included in this chapter with the following individual: William Gross.

A quotation was also drawn from *Our Cosmic Habitat*, p. 83.

Chapter One

Between February and October 2003, the author conducted interviews included in this chapter with the following individual: W. Gross.

Between February and May 2003, the author conducted interviews included in this chapter with the following individuals:
Benjamin Ehlert
William Podlich

Between May and August 2003, the author conducted interviews included in this chapter with the following individuals:
James Muzzy
Walter Gerken
William Thompson
Mark Kiesel
Chris Dialynas

In October 2003, the author conducted interviews included in this chapter with the following individual: Kelly Minadur, The Foundation Center.

Chapter Two

Between February and October 2003, the author conducted interviews included in this chapter with the following individual: W. Gross.

Between May and October 2003, the author conducted interviews included in this chapter with the following individuals:
Scott Simon
M. Kiesel

Information on Fidelity Magellan and other mutual funds is taken from Morningstar Principia Pro software, releases for June through October 2003.

All unattributed information about the bond market was provided by members of the PIMCO research department.

Warren Buffett Way, pp. 1–26

Chapter Three

Between February and October 2003, the author conducted interviews included in this chapter with the following individual: W. Gross.

Secondary sources consulted included:
Bill Gross on Investing, throughout
Reminiscences of a Stock Operator, throughout
Jesse Livermore, throughout
Morgan: American Financier, chiefly pp. 2–166
The House of Morgan, pp. 3–161
Baruch, throughout

Wall Street: A History, pp. 35–151
Wall Street People, pp. 33–51, 224–235

Chapter Four

Between February and October 2003, the author conducted interviews included in this chapter with the following individuals:
W. Gross
Paul McCulley

The author attended the PIMCO Secular Forum May 5–7, 2003, in Newport Beach, California. The information described in the book was drawn from oral and written presentations and interchanges at this meeting.

Chapter Five

Between February and October 2003, the author conducted interviews included in this chapter with the following individuals:
W. Gross
P. McCulley

Between February and August 2003, the author conducted interviews included in this chapter with the following individuals:
Jim Keller
John Brynjolfsson
Ray Kennedy

Information about bond ratings were taken from the web sites of Moody's Investors Service (*moodys.com*) and Standard & Poor's Corp. (*standardandpoors.com*).

Information about closed-end funds was drawn from the PIMCO research staff and two web sites, *ETFconnect.com*, a service of John Nuveen, and *cefa.com*, the official site of the Closed-End Fund Association.

Chapter Six

Between February and October 2003, the author conducted interviews included in this chapter with the following individuals:
W. Gross
Mark McCray

News reported, such as on the tobacco Master Settlement Agreement, taken from published accounts in the *New York Times*, *Wall Street Journal*, *Barron's*, etc.

Closed-end fund information taken from *ETFConnect.com*.

Tax rates taken from the Federation of Tax Administrators' web site, *taxadmin.org*.

Chapter Seven

Between February and October 2003, the author conducted interviews included in this chapter with the following individuals:
    W. Gross
    Mohamed El-Erian
    Sudi Mariappa
    Mark Porterfield

In October 2003, the author also conducted interviews included in this chapter with Tom McCool of the federal General Accounting Office for information about the total cost of the 1980s savings and loan crisis.

Information about economies of emerging markets countries was taken from *The Economist Pocket World in Figures*, 2003.

Information about Lehman Brothers bond indices was taken from the company's web site, *lehmanlive.com*.

Chapter Eight

Between February and October 2003, the author conducted interviews included in this chapter with the following individuals:
    W. Gross
    J. Brynjolfsson

Chapter Nine

Between February and October 2003, the author conducted interviews included in this chapter with the following individual: W. Gross.

All of the conclusions and recommendations are those of the author.

Bibliography

Baruch, Bernard M. *My Own Story*. New York: Henry Holt & Co., 1957. Reprinted by Buccaneer Books Inc., Cutchogue, NY.

Berlin, Sir Isaiah. *The Hedgehog and the Fox: An Essay on Tolstoy's View of History*. New York: Simon & Schuster, 1953.

Chancellor, Edward. *Devil Take the Hindmost: A History of Financial Speculation*. New York: Penguin Putnam, 1999.

Chernow, Ron. *The House of Morgan: An American Banking Dynasty and the Rise of Modern Finance*. New York: Touchstone, 1991.

The Economist Pocket World in Figures, 2003. London: Profile Books, 2002.

Ellis, Charles D., and James R. Vertin. *Wall Street People, Vol. 2*. New York: John Wiley & Sons, 2003.

Geisst, Charles R. *Wall Street: A History*. New York: Oxford University Press, 1997.

Greider, William. *One World, Ready or Not: The Manic Logic of Global Capitalism*. New York: Simon & Shuster, 1997.

Greider, William. *Secrets of the Temple: How the Federal Reserve Runs the Country*. New York: Simon & Schuster, 1987.

Greider, William. *Who Will Tell The People: The Betrayal of American Democracy.* New York: Simon & Shuster, 1992.

Gross, William H. *Bill Gross on Investing.* New York: John Wiley & Sons, 1997–1998. [Previously published as *Everything You've Heard About Investing is Wrong!* New York: Times Books, 1997.]

Gross, William H. *30 Years and Counting: A Select Collection of Bill Gross' Investment Outlooks Accompanied by His Most Recent.* Newport Beach, CA: Pacific Investment Management Company, 2003.

Hagstrom, Robert G. *The Warren Buffett Way.* New York: John Wiley & Sons, 1997.

Lefèvre, Edwin. *Reminiscences of a Stock Operator.* New York: John Wiley & Sons, 1993. [Originally published in 1923 by George H. Duran & Co.]

Livermore, Jesse Lauriston. *How to Trade in Stocks: The Livermore Formula for Combining Time Element and Price.* New York: Duel, Sloan & Pearce, 1940. Out of print; reissued in 2001, commented on and edited by Richard Smitten. Greenville, SC: Traders Press.

Phillips, Kevin P. *The Emerging Republican Majority.* New Rochelle, N.Y.: Arlington House, 1969.

Phillips, Kevin P. *The Politics of Rich and Poor: Wealth and the American Electorate in the Reagan Aftermath.* New York: Random House, 1990.

Phillips, Kevin P. *Wealth and Democracy: A Political History of the American Rich.* New York: Broadway Books, 2002.

Rees, Martin. *Our Cosmic Habitat.* Princeton, NJ: Princeton University Press, 2001.

Rosenberg, Claude N. Jr. *Investing With the Best: What to Look For, What to Look Out For in Your Search for a Superior Investment Manager,* 2nd ed. New York: John Wiley & Sons, 1993.

Smitten, Richard. *Jesse Livermore: World's Greatest Stock Trader.* New York: John Wiley & Sons, 2001.

Strouse, Jean. *Morgan: American Financier.* New York: Perennial, 2000. [Previously published in 1999 by Random House Inc.]

Temel, Judy Wesalo. *The Fundamentals of Municipal Bonds,* 5th ed. New York: John Wiley & Sons, 2001.

Thorpe, Edward O. *Beat the Dealer.* New York: Random House, Rev. ed. 1966.

Index